Writing to Learn
THE PARAGRAPH

10:30 — 1:00

3:00 — 5:30

Writing to Learn
THE PARAGRAPH

LOU J. SPAVENTA
MARILYNN L. SPAVENTA

Santa Barbara City College

Boston   Burr Ridge, IL   Dubuque, IA   Madison, WI   New York   San Francisco   St. Louis
Bangkok   Bogotá   Caracas   Kuala Lumpur   Lisbon   London   Madrid   Mexico City
Milan   Montreal   New Delhi   Santiago   Seoul   Singapore   Sydney   Taipei   Toronto

McGraw-Hill Higher Education

A Division of The **McGraw-Hill** *Companies*

WRITING TO LEARN: THE PARAGRAPH
International Edition 2001

Exclusive rights by McGraw-Hill Book Co – Singapore, for manufacture and export. This book cannot be re-exported from the country to which it is sold by McGraw-Hill. The International Edition is not available in North America.

10 09 08 07 06 05 04 03 02 01
20 09 08 07 06 05 04 03 02 01
PMP   SEP

Library of Congress Cataloging-in-Publication Data
Spaventa, Louis J.
  Writing to learn / Louis J. Spaventa, Marilynn L. Spaventa. – 1st ed.
  Includes indexes.
  Contents: [bk. 1] The sentence – bk. 2. The paragraph – bk. 3. From paragraph to essay -- bk. 4. The essay.
ISBN 0-07-230753-6 (bk.1) – ISBN 0-07-230754-4 (bk2.) – ISBN 0-07-230775-2 (bk. 3) – ISBN 0-07-230756-0 (bk. 4)
  2.   English language—Textbooks for foreign speakers. 2. English language—Rhetoric—Problems, exercises, etc. 3. Report writing—Problems, exercises, etc. I. Spaventa, Marilynn. II. Title.
PE1128.S697   2000
808'.042—dc21   99-057820
                                                                              CIP

www.mhhe.com

When ordering this title, use ISBN 0-07-118829-0

Printed in Singapore

CONTENTS

Unit One: Myself and Others
Chapter 1

Chapter 12

PREFACE

To the Instructor

WRITING TO LEARN is a four-book ESL writing series aimed at adult learners of English from diverse educational backgrounds. The series focuses both on the process of writing and on writing as a product. The goal of the series is to help students learn how to write for academic and vocational success. Each book in the series makes use of student skills and experience to generate writing topics while providing guided practice of appropriate vocabulary and grammar, English writing conventions, writing, editing, rewriting, and journal writing. Each chapter of the first three books in the series begins with a visual image that leads to discussion and writing. The fourth text uses photographs and readings as prewriting prompts. WRITING TO LEARN begins with an elementary text designed to improve student ability to write accurate and descriptive English sentences. The upper elementary to intermediate level text focuses on writing paragraphs. The third or intermediate level text takes the student from paragraph writing to organizing, writing, and editing essays. The final book at the advanced level concentrates on improving student essay writing skills and enhancing essay writing style.

Each book in the series is divided into six units. Books 1 and 2, *The Sentence* and *The Paragraph,* have two chapters in each unit while books 3 and 4, *From Paragraph to Essay* and *Writing Essays,* have just six units each. The reason for the difference is to create more and shorter lessons for the elementary to lower intermediate levels, and fewer but longer lessons at the intermediate to advanced levels of writing.

Here are the unit themes:

Unit One: Myself and Others

Unit Two: Family and Relationships

Unit Three: Education

Unit Four: Work

Unit Five: Leisure and Recreation

Unit Six: The Natural World

Students who work through several texts in the series will have the opportunity to explore the same theme from different perspectives.

The use of icons to indicate pair and group work ⟨2⟩ ⟨4⟩ ⟨CLASS⟩ is meant to facilitate classroom organization while eliminating repetitive instructions. Notice that the number indicates the total number of students needed to form the group. Be sure to follow each chapter in the Instructor's Edition for helpful suggestions and instructions for activities that are not included in the student text.

Organization

Each unit and chapter is divided into the following four sections:

A. Prewriting   In *The Paragraph,* each chapter begins with prewriting activities based on a picture story. Prewriting activities include vocabulary learning, pair work, group work, and discussion. It is important to begin writing lessons with something to talk about and the words necessary to talk. We encourage a lot of conversation before the student writes.

B. Structure   Grammar activities include review of the basic English grammar necessary for the writing in the chapter. While the structure section introduces grammar with example, explanation, and practice exercises, *The Paragraph* is not meant to be a grammar text. Grammar has been incorporated as a tool for expressing one's thoughts rather than as an end in itself.

C. Writing and Editing   Activities in this section are devoted to improving writing skills, especially employing the vocabulary and grammar practiced in sections A and B. Activities in this section develop from controlled to creative practice. You will notice that we have not included sample student sentences and paragraphs for students to follow in the writing section. In many texts, writing samples are provided with the expectation that students will diligently work with the sample to produce their own personalized writing. In fact, this rarely happens and students are more likely to be constricted by the model. In this series, the writing models appear in the structure and editing sections to encourage students to alter the samples and make the language their own.

D. Journal Assignment   The personal, unedited, daily writing practice that journal writing affords is an important part of the process of writing well in English. To introduce students to journal writing, there is a journal writing assignment at the end of each chapter in this second book. Other texts in the series provide more extensive lists of topics. These assignments allow students to synthesize and expand what they are studying in each unit.

You will need to decide how you will respond to student journal writing. Here are a few suggestions.

- Respond only to the content of what is written in the journal.

- Look for positive examples of vocabulary and grammar usage consistent with each chapter and highlight or underline them in student journals.

- Tell students you are going to read their journals with an eye toward a particular kind of writing: a descriptive sentence, an opinion, a comparison, an analysis or explanation, and so on. Then identify that writing when you come across it in student journals.

- Ask students to read something from their journals during class time. Ask the students listening to respond in writing to what they hear.

- Each week, read selected journal entries aloud to the entire class to inspire and foster respect among students of each other as writers.

Appendices   Each text contains appendices of grammar and writing conventions for student reference. During your first class meeting, when you familiarize students with the book, make sure you take some time to point out the appendices and what they contain. Students too often discover appendices at the end of a course.

Instructor's Edition   The Instructor's Edition of *The Paragraph* contains chapter-by-chapter notes of explanation, advice, suggestions, and reproducible quizzes for each chapter.

Web Site   The *Writing to Learn* web site can be located through The McGraw-Hill, Inc. web site at <www.mhhe.com> This interactive site should be useful to instructors and students. For instructors, the site can be a virtual teacher's room, where instructors can raise questions and exchange ideas and activities related to this series. Students can post and read writing assignments for each chapter and thus expand the walls of their classroom.

The Paragraph

This second book in the series emphasizes writing paragraphs. Picture stories are used to elicit vocabulary, discussion, and student opinion. The instructor will find it easy to order sentences into a paragraph based on the picture sequence in each chapter if he or she chooses to do so. Some exercises in the book involving manipulation of language within a paragraph give students the opportunity to work with paragraphs. However, student success in using this book should be based on ability to create a meaningful paragraph from the beginning step of brainstorming information to redrafting for style, grammaticality, effect on the reader, and content. So while one goal of the text is to expose students to the form of the English paragraph, another goal is to give them some thinking tools to use in creating their own paragraphs.

The First Lesson

Begin your first class with an exercise that helps your students become familiar with this text. You can do this orally, in writing, or both. Students might work in pairs or small groups. A familiarization exercise is contained in the **To the Student** part of the introduction to *The Paragraph*.

Question your students about the names of the six units, the number of chapters in each unit, the number of sections in each chapter, the number and names of the appendices, and their thoughts about the use of each chapter section and appendix. Create and distribute a follow-up activity that reviews the text organization.

If you do the exercise orally, use the cooperative question-and-answer technique called "Numbered heads together." Have each student in a pair or group count off: 1, 2 or 1, 2, 3, 4. Tell the class that before you call on anyone to answer, students who know the answer in a pair or group should tell the answer to their partner or group mates. Then pick a number. When you call "Number 1," for example, only students who are "Number 1" may raise their hands to answer. If the answer is correct, go on to the next question. If it is not, ask another "Number 1." In this way, you can begin teaching students to rely on their partners or group mates. We encourage students to turn to each other as resources for language learning. This is an essential element of process writing.

Acknowledgments

First and foremost, we acknowledge the debt of thanks we owe to our students at Santa Barbara City College, whose interests and concerns were the catalyst that led us to embark upon this writing project. We would like to thank as well our colleagues at City College and in the larger field of ESOL writing, who often made valuable suggestions to us about our manuscripts.

This book and this series would not have been written without the encouragement and persistence of Tim Stookesberry and Aurora Martinez, at McGraw-Hill, and of our series editor, the inimitable, indefatigable, and empathetic Bob Hemmer.

Should you have any suggestions or comments, we would be happy to receive them from you in writing, via email, or at our web site. You can write to us care of the ESL Department, Santa Barbara City College, Santa Barbara, California, 93109, USA. Our email address is spaventa@sbcc.net.

Lou and Marilynn Spaventa
Santa Barbara, California

To the Student

Welcome to *The Paragraph!*

The goal of this book is to help you write good English paragraphs. The book has six units. Each unit has a topic. You will discuss the topic. You will write about the topic. The topic for Unit One is Myself and Others. Look for the topics of the other units. Look in the Contents. Write the names of the topics below.

Unit One   <u>Myself and Others</u>

Unit Two   _____

Unit Three   _____

Unit Four   _____

Unit Five   _____

Unit Six   _____

Now look at Unit One. How many chapters are there?

If you said "two," you are right. Each unit has two chapters. How many chapters are there in the book? Your answer _____

Take five minutes to skim (look quickly) through the chapters. Look only at the first page of each chapter. Then close the book. Write down whatever words come into your mind. Write down words about what you saw.

_____

_____

_____

Each chapter has four sections. Match the section with its description. Draw a line from the section to its description.

Section	Description
Prewriting	gives ideas for writing on your own in a journal
Structure	practices English grammar
Writing and Editing	prepares you for writing by learning vocabulary and giving ideas to discuss
Journal Assignment	has exercises to improve your writing skills

Your instructor will decide how to use this book in the best way for you. Please write in this book. Write words and sentences. We designed *The Paragraph* as a workbook. The book is for reading and writing. So please write in it.

Now you have met our book *The Paragraph.* Your Instructor may ask you some questions about the book. Be prepared to answer them. We hope you enjoy working with the book. Remember that learning to write well is a skill. You need to practice a skill to improve. Write a lot. Write what you feel and what you think. Learn a lot!

Lou and Marilynn Spaventa

Writing to Learn
THE PARAGRAPH

Myself and Others

A Prewriting

Exercise 1. Thinking of words   Look at each picture on page 3. Write all the words you know for each picture. Write on the pictures. Do not write on the lines yet.

Exercise 2. Reading and writing the story   Read the sentences that follow. Write the correct sentence on the line under each picture on page 3.

I couldn't find my bags.

I couldn't find my ticket and passport.

We had a flat tire. I almost missed my plane.

I woke up late.

There was a lot of fog. The plane couldn't land.

Nobody talked to me on the plane.

Exercise 3. Choosing a title   Choose the title that follows the rules for title form. Write it on page 3.

Rules for Writing Titles

- Always begin the first word in a title with a capital letter.

- Use a capital letter for the first letter of each important word in a title.

- Don't use a capital letter for small words like **a, an, the** (articles); **to, for, from** (prepositions); **and, but, so, or** (conjunctions).

- Don't use a period at the end of a title.

---

a TERRIBLE TRIP.

A terrible trip

A Terrible Trip

1.

2.

3.

4.

5.

6. BAGGAGE CLAIM

Exercise 4. Writing in paragraph form   Now rewrite the story from page 2 about Young Cho's terrible trip in paragraph form.

My trip was terrible. First of all, _____.

On the way to the airport, _____.

_____. At the airport I had another

problem. _____. My trip didn't get better

on the airplane. _____. When we arrived,

_____. _____.

To end my terrible experience, _____.

What a nightmare!

Exercise 5. Thinking of words   Look at each picture. Write all the words you know for each picture. Write on the pictures. Do not write on the lines yet.

party _____   wake up

1.   *My friends had a good*
   —bye party for me.

2.   *I woke up*
   early

Unit 1: Myself and Others

leave

3. GATE 12

talking

4.

My family and friends came to the airport with me   I practiced English with my new friend Johnny.

arrive

5. BAGGAGE CLAIM

visit his family

6.

I was lucky. I found my suitcases easily   My uncle and cousin were waiting for me

Exercise 6. Reading and writing the story Read the sentences that follow. Write the correct sentence on the lines under each picture.

My family and friends came to the airport with me.

My uncle and cousin were waiting for me.

I was lucky. I found my suitcases easily.

I practiced English with my new friend, Johnny.

My friends had a good-bye party for me.

I woke up early.

Exercise 7. Writing a title Choose a word to complete the title for this story.

My _____ Trip

Wonderful

Terrible

Perfect

Write the title in the space on page 4.

Exercise 8. Writing in paragraph form Now rewrite the story from pages 4–5 in paragraph form.

~~My perfect Trip~~

My trip to the United States was ___perfect___ _____. The night before I left, ~~party for me, my frien~~. That morning, ~~I woke up early~~ . ~~My family good-bye~~. On the plane, ~~I'm talking with my friend~~. When we landed, ~~we arrive and ful my bag easily~~ ~~My cousin and uncle waiting for me.~~ were

B   Structure

Exercise 1. Using *a* and *an* In both preceding sets of pictures, there are many different things. For example, there is an alarm clock. There is also a young man. Say the following words out loud. Then write **a** or **an** in front of the word.

Spelling and Pronunciation Rule

Use *an* before a word whose first sound is a vowel sound. In all other cases, use *a*.

EXAMPLE: **a** young man

an airline

_____ car	_____ woman	_____ highway
_____ sign	_____ airplane	_____ agent
_____ aisle	_____ airport	_____ hour
_____ house	_____ old man	_____ easy word
_____ U-turn	_____ underpass	_____ engine
_____ wing	_____ exit	_____ information counter

Exercise 2. What's in the pictures? Using *there is* and *there are* To tell someone what we see in a place or what we know is in a place, use **there is** or **there are.** Use **there is** with singular nouns and **there are** with plural nouns.

> **EXAMPLE:** There is an alarm clock on the table.
>
> There are many cars on the highway.

Complete the following sentences using **there is** or **there are.**

1. _____ a young man putting on his clothes.

2. _____ three people in a car.

3. _____ a ticket agent behind the counter.

4. _____ many people on the plane.

5. _____ a plane circling the airport.

6. _____ only one bag left in the Baggage Claim Area.

Exercise 3. More practice with *there is* and *there are* When there is more than one noun in a sentence, use **is** if the first noun is singular. Use **are** if the first noun is plural.

> **EXAMPLE:** There is a girl and two boys.
>
> There are three suitcases.

Complete the following sentences with **there is** or **there are.**

1. _____ two men and a woman in that car.

2. _____ a plane and many cars in the picture.

3. _____ pillows and a blanket on the bed.

4. _____ a plane in the air and two planes on the ground.

5. _____ only one ticket agent and a long line of people.

6. _____ several people with bags and one person without bags.

Chapter 1

Exercise 4. Practicing pronouns Read about Young Cho's bad dream again. Rewrite Young Cho's paragraph. Change **I** to **he.** Change all of the pronouns. Don't forget to change the verb forms, too.

My Terrible Trip

My trip was terrible. First of all, I woke up late. On the way to the airport, we had a flat tire. I almost missed my plane. At the airport I had another problem. I couldn't find my ticket and passport. My trip didn't get better on the airplane. Nobody talked to me on the plane. When we arrived, there was a lot of fog. The plane couldn't land. To end my terrible experience, I couldn't find my bags. What a nightmare!

Pronoun Review

Subject Pronouns		Possessive Pronouns		Object Pronouns	
I	we	my	our	me	us
you	you	your	your	you	you
he/she/it	they	his/her/its	their	him/her/it	them

Young Cho's Terrible Trip

His trip was terrible. He _____

_____

_____

_____

_____

_____

Now read the story out loud to a partner. Your partner can practice reading to you, too. Finally, look only at the pictures on pages 4–5 and retell the story using **Young-Cho** and **he.**

Exercise 5. Reviewing the verb *be* in the present tense Complete these sentences using the verb **be** in the present tense. Also, change the boldfaced nouns to pronouns.

The Verb *Be*—Present Tense

I am	we are
you are	you are
he, she, it is	they are

EXAMPLE: **Young Cho** / Korean. He is Korean.

1. **Young Cho** / a student

   _____

2. **His parents** / sad because **Young Cho** is leaving

   _____

3. **The airport** / crowded

   _____

4. **Many people** / on line

   _____

5. **Young Cho and I** / second language students

   _____

6. **The food** / not good

   _____

Exercise 6. Reviewing the verb *be* in the past tense   Complete these sentences using the correct past tense form of the verb **be**. Also change the boldfaced nouns to pronouns.

The Verb *Be*—Past Tense

I was	we were
you were	you were
he, she, it was	they were

EXAMPLE: **Young Cho** / late yesterday. He was late yesterday.

1. **His friends** / at his party

_____

2. **His sister** / interested in going to America with **Young Cho**

_____

3. **His parents** / sad to say good-bye

_____

4. **His suitcase and his carry-on bag** / very heavy

_____

5. **His cat** / at the window when he left

_____

6. **His flight** / delayed

_____

Exercise 7. Choosing the correct tense with the verb *be* Read the following sentences carefully and write in the correct present or past tense form of the verb **be.**

Mary _____ very tired today because she _____ up very late last night. Even her parents _____ asleep when she came home. Her friends had a big celebration. All of her friends from high school _____ at the restaurant when she arrived with her best friend Cecilia. It _____ a surprise party!

Today she _____ exhausted. Her parents _____ sad to say good-bye but happy that she _____ on her way for a great adventure. All of the friends who _____ at the party last night _____ sleeping happily in their beds now.

C Writing and Editing

Exercise 1. Brainstorming Think about *your* trip here. In the following box, write down all of the words that come into your head. Do not try to write complete sentences yet. Write only words.

EXAMPLE:

sad	big suitcase
rain	nervous

Exercise 2. Organizing ideas Draw pictures that tell about your trip. You don't need to be an artist. You can draw simple pictures to show your ideas.

EXAMPLE:

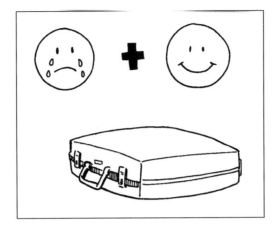

Tell your group about your pictures. Ask questions about the pictures of the other students in your group.

Unit 1: Myself and Others

Exercise 3. Choosing a title   Choose one word to describe your trip. Use one of these words or choose another. Then write the word in the title and topic sentence.

Terrible   Wonderful   Sad   Exciting   Bittersweet

My _____ Trip

My trip here was _____.

Exercise 4. Writing a paragraph   Use your ideas from Exercises 1, 2, and 3 to write your paragraph here.

M y _____ T r i p

My trip was _____

_____

_____

_____

_____

_____

_____

_____

_____

Read your paragraph carefully. Make changes and corrections.

Exercise 5. Editing   Read your partner's paragraph and answer the following questions about it.

Editing checklist for _____'s paragraph
(name of your partner)

What is one word that describes your partner's trip? _____

Can you understand the story?

_____ Yes

_____ Yes, but one part is confusing

_____ No

Do all of the sentences start with capital letters?

_____ Yes

_____ No

Do all sentences end with a period (.) or a question mark (?) ?

_____ Yes

_____ No

D   Journal Assignment

Write in your journal on one of these topics.

- My favorite trip in my childhood
- A trip I want to take
- What I brought when I came here
- A typical day
- An unusual day
- A memorable day

Myself and Others

A Prewriting

Exercise 1. Vocabulary word search Look at the first picture. Tell the other students all the words you know. Write the words on the picture. Don't be afraid to write in this book. If you write a word on the picture, you will remember it better. Do this for all four pictures.

Then choose two words from each picture. Write a sentence beside the picture for each word you have chosen.

EXAMPLE: receptionist

A receptionist answers the telephone.

1. _____

    _____

2. _____

    _____

3. _____

    _____

4. _____

    _____

5. _____

   _____

6. _____

   _____

7. _____

   _____

8. _____

   _____

Exercise 2. Working with the alphabet   Often when we give our name to someone, we need to spell it out. Look at the alphabet below. It is the American English alphabet. There is a key word to help you pronounce each letter.

A, a	say		**N, n**	ten
B, b	bee		**O, o**	oh
C, c	see		**P, p**	pea
D, d	deep		**Q, q**	cue
E, e	eat		**R, r**	car
F, f	if		**S, s**	yes
G, g	gee		**T, t**	tea
H, h	each		**U, u**	you
I, i	eye		**V, v**	visa
J, j	jay		**W, w**	double you
K, k	Kay		**X, x**	Texas
L, l	sell		**Y, y**	why
M, m	them		**Z, z**	zebra

Use your notebook and pen for the next activity. Stand up. Walk around the room. Ask a classmate what his or her name is. When you hear it, say "How do you spell it?" Write each name below. Remember to listen and then write.

1. _____

2. _____

3. _____

4. _____

5. _____

6. _____

7. _____

8. _____

9. _____

10. _____

Exercise 3. Where are they?   María Brown and Marie Brown are sitting. They are waiting for someone. Read the dialogue and look at the picture story on pages 16–17 again. Where do you think they are? Why do you think they are waiting? Write down all the answers you can think of. Ask your teacher for help if you do not know the word to explain your idea.

Where are they? _____

Why are they waiting? (Be specific) _____

Now share your answers with a classmate. Decide on one answer for both of you. Complete the sentence that follows.

We think they are waiting _____

Exercise 4. Retelling the first part of the story   Use the following outline to help you retell the first part of the story. First practice telling the story to a partner. Then write the story.

Two women with similar _____ were waiting _____. The

receptionist called out, "_____." Both women _____. Then

the receptionist asked, "_____."

Exercise 5. Finding something in common   The coincidence in this story is that the two women have similar names. They have something in common.

   Find out what you have in common with your classmates. Maybe you have similar names. Possibly you come from the same city. Maybe you like the same kind of music. Maybe you have the same color eyes.

Walk around the room. Look at your classmates. Ask questions to find similarities.

EXAMPLES: Do you like hip hop?

Are you a good cook?

Write six similarities below.

EXAMPLES: Jean and I like hip hop music. **or** Juan and I are good cooks.

1. _____

2. _____

3. _____

4. _____

5. _____

6. _____

B Structure

Exercise 1. Review of present continuous tense   Look around the classroom. Look at your classmates. Write five sentences about your classmates. Write the sentences in Column A on page 20.

EXAMPLES: Juan is sitting in the first seat.

Tri and Ana are writing in their books.

Present Continuous Tense

Present tense of **be** + **-ing** form of the verb

    I am working.   We are working.

    You are working.   You are working.

    He/She/It is working.   They are working.

Use the present continuous (progressive) tense for actions happening *now* or at the time of speaking or writing. See Appendix III on page 147 for spelling rules.

Column A	Column B
1. _____	1. _____
_____	_____
2. _____	2. _____
_____	_____
3. _____	3. _____
_____	_____
4. _____	4. _____
_____	_____
5. _____	5. _____
_____	_____

Exercise 2. Asking questions with *who*   Read your sentences from Exercise 1 to a classmate. After you read the sentence, ask your classmate a question with **who.** Take turns asking and answering questions. Don't write. Just practice speaking.

EXAMPLE: Who is sitting in the first seat?

POSSIBLE ANSWERS: Juan is sitting in the first seat.

Juan is.

Juan.

Exercise 3. Writing another sentence to describe your classmates   Look at the sentences you wrote in Exercise 1. Look at your classmates again. Look at the same people. Write another sentence about each one. Write it in Exercise 1, Column B.

Here are some questions to help you: *What is he or she wearing? What is he or she doing? What do you know about him or her?*

EXAMPLES: Juan is wearing a T-shirt.

Juan is smiling at me.

Tri and Ana are taking a tennis class together.

Exercise 4. Combining sentences and asking questions   You can combine two sentences so that your writing flows better. Notice that the sentences have the same subject, *Juan.* You do not need to repeat the subject. You do not need to repeat the **be** part of the verb.

> **EXAMPLE:** Juan **is sitting** in the first seat. Juan is wearing a T-shirt.
> Juan **is sitting** in the first seat and **wearing** a T-shirt.

You can also ask a question with **who** like this: *Who is sitting in the first seat and wearing a T-shirt?* Rewrite the two sentences in Columns A and B, Exercise 1 into one sentence. Write the sentences below.

1. _____

2. _____

3. _____

4. _____

5. _____

C   Writing and Editing

Exercise 1. Talking about the picture story   Tell the story of Marie Brown and María Brown together with your classmates. Use your imagination to add new details. As your classmates speak, write down some of the important words they say.

> **EXAMPLE:** The women were waiting in an office.
> women, waiting, office

Exercise 2. Writing a collaborative story   Use your notes from Exercise 1 to help write the story. Choose a recorder for your group. (A recorder is a person who writes things down.) Talk about the best sentences to tell the story. Tell the recorder what to write. There should be at least five sentences in your group story.

   When the story is finished, put it on the classroom wall or blackboard. Walk around the room and read the stories from other groups. If you think something in a story needs to change, write your change over it with a pencil.

Exercise 3. Editing your story   Take your story down from the wall or blackboard. Read it again. Discuss any changes. If there are no changes, then each person in the group should copy the story. If there are changes, make them. Then copy the story. Write it below.

Exercise 4. Writing a title   Read the story again. Think about a good title. Write down two or three titles. Show them to your partner. Choose one title. Write it above your story.

D Journal Assignment

Here are some topics to write about in your journal. Find a quiet comfortable place. Choose a topic. Don't use a dictionary. Write for ten minutes. Don't stop.

- A coincidence I had
- How people confuse my name
- I am like my classmates
- How I got my name
- I am different from my classmates
- Differences between names in my culture and names in this culture

UNIT TWO
CHAPTER 3

Family and Relationships

A   Prewriting

1.

2.

3.

4.

Exercise 1. Talking about a picture   Each person in the group should speak about one picture on page 24. First, say what you see and what you think about the people in the picture. Then, after everyone speaks, try to connect the pictures into one story. Write down new words and important words in the box that follows.

New Words / Important Words

Exercise 2. Brainstorming words about the family   Make a list of all the words you know about family relationships, for example, *father, brother-in-law, cousin.* Write the words below.

_____

_____

_____

_____

_____

Now return to your group of four from Exercise 1. Compare the two lists of words. Check spelling.

Exercise 3. Creating a spelling dictation   Choose ten words from your lists from Exercise 2 to dictate to another group. Then choose one person to dictate the words. (A person from the other group will dictate words to your group.) The dictation will be by spelling. For example, someone says "f-a-t-h-e-r" and you write **father.**

   Write the words below. Use the letter pronunciation guide on page 17 if you need help.

1. _____

2. _____

3. _____

4. _____

5. _____

6. _____

7. _____

8. _____

9. _____

10. _____

Exercise 4. Writing sentences   Choose five words from Exercise 3. Write sentences about your family with these words.

> **EXAMPLE:** parents
> My parents live in Buenos Aires.

1. _____

2. _____

3. _____

4. _____

5. _____

Exercise 5. Preparing to speak in front of others   Bring a picture of your family to class. If you don't have a picture, then make a drawing or cut out pictures from a magazine. Prepare this the day before you speak.

At home, practice speaking about your family for three minutes without stopping. Tell what their names are. Tell how old they are. Tell what they do. Tell what they like. Tell other interesting information about them. If you can, it helps to practice in front of a mirror. Make some notes to help you speak. Notes are just important words and phrases you want to remember. Do not write a whole story in complete sentences.

Notes

Exercise 6. **Speaking in front of others about your family**   Each person in the group takes a turn speaking. The others listen. One person is the timer. That person says "time" after two minutes. Each listener should ask the speaker one question.

B   Structure

 ### Exercise 1. Spelling comparative adjectives

> Words like **old, young, tall** and **short** describe people, things, and situations. They are called *adjectives*. To compare two people, things, or situations, add **-er** to the one-syllable adjectives. Here is an example comparing two people.
>
> **EXAMPLE:** Mia is faster than Michael.

Make comparative adjectives by adding **-er** to the word. These words have one syllable.

1. tall _____   5. short _____

2. small _____   6. bright _____

3. smart _____   7. slow _____

4. young _____   8. old _____

> Two-syllable adjectives that end in the letter **y** require a spelling change. Change the **y** to **i.** Then add **er.**
>
> **EXAMPLE:** happy + **er**
>
>   happier

Write the comparative form of these adjectives.

1. healthy _____   3. lazy _____

2. easy _____   4. noisy _____

One- and two-syllable adjectives that end in **b, d, f, g, m, n, p, s,** and **t** double the final letter if the last two letters of the adjective are a vowel followed by a consonant.

EXAMPLE: big + **er**

bigger

Write the comparative form of these adjectives.

1. thin   _____   3. sad   _____

2. wet   _____   4. mad   _____

If the adjective ends in the letter **e,** just add **r.**

EXAMPLE: pure + **er**

purer

Write the comparative form of these adjectives.

1. safe   _____   3. free   _____

2. brave   _____   4. close   _____

If the adjective has two syllables or more and does not end in **y,** do not use **er.** Use the word **more** before the adjective.

EXAMPLE: beautiful

more beautiful

Write the comparative form of these adjectives.

1. helpful   _____   3. exciting   _____

2. interested   _____   4. dangerous   _____

Exercise 2. Comparing yourself with people in your family   How do you compare with the other people in your family? With your brothers or sisters? With your mother and father? With your grandparents, aunts, and uncles?

EXAMPLE: I am 21. My brother is 16.
I am older than my brother is.

My brother is 16. I am 21.
My brother is younger than I am.

Now think of the people in your family. Think of yourself. How do you compare with them? Write five sentences below.

1. _____
2. _____
3. _____
4. _____
5. _____

Exercise 3. Comparing your family with a classmate's family   Read your sentences from Exercise 2 to your partner. Listen to his or her sentences. Then compare your families. You do not need to write the sentences.

EXAMPLE: Juan: I am shorter than my brother Luis.
Hiromi: I am shorter than my sister Mariko.
Juan: How tall is Mariko?
Hiromi: 165 centimeters.
Juan: Then my brother Luis is taller than your sister Mariko. He's 180 centimeters.

Exercise 4. Writing about the picture story   Turn back to the story on page 24. Write sentences comparing the people in the pictures. Use your imagination to add interesting information.

1. _____
2. _____
3. _____
4. _____
5. _____
6. _____

Now take turns reading sentences. If you hear a new word or a sentence you don't understand, ask the person to repeat it.

Chapter 3

29

Exercise 5. Comparing yourself with your classmates   On a piece of paper, write a sentence comparing yourself with one of your classmates. Do not write your name on the paper.

EXAMPLE: I am funnier than Romero.

Give the paper to your teacher. The teacher will read the sentences. Try to guess who wrote each sentence. Write five of the sentences below. Write sentences you like.

1. _____

2. _____

3. _____

4. _____

5. _____

C   Writing and Editing

Exercise 1. Taking notes to prepare for writing   Speak for three minutes about yourself. Speak about the things you like to do. The listener should take notes. After the first partner speaks, the other should ask questions from the notes. Then switch roles.

Notes
ʳ |3

Exercise 2. Writing comparisons based on your notes Use your notes from Exercise 1. Write five sentences comparing yourself and your partner.

      EXAMPLE: Ki Sung, 29, three sisters / me, 27, two sisters
              Ki Sung is two years older than I am.
              Ki Sung has one more sister than I have.

1. _____

2. _____

3. _____

4. _____

5. _____

Exercise 3. Writing a first draft paragraph You are ready to write a first draft paragraph. Your topic is a comparison of you and your partner. For the title, just add your classmate's name in the space that follows. Think of a sentence to introduce your ideas. This is called the topic sentence.

_____ and I

_____
(Topic sentence)

_____
(Body of paragraph*)

_____

_____

_____

_____

_____

_____

_____

* Your sentences from Exercise 2 and other sentences.

Exercise 4. Getting oral feedback   Read your paragraph to your group. Don't show it to your group. Just read it. Read as clearly as you can. You may need to slow down a little when you read. You may also need to ask for help with pronunciation. After you read, ask your group these questions. Write the answers below each one.

1. What did you understand?

_____

2. What is something more you want to know?

_____

3. Is there something in the story I should take out?

_____

What?

_____

4. What did you like best in my story?

_____

Now go back to Exercise 3. Use your group mates' feedback to make changes in your draft paragraph.

Exercise 5. Adding a final sentence (conclusion)   Most paragraphs end with a conclusion. The conclusion is usually the last sentence in the paragraph. It retells the main ideas in your writing. Here is a sample paragraph. Read it. Then write a conclusion. After you write it, compare your conclusion with a partner's conclusion.

Two Very Different People

Joachim comes from Germany. I come from Brazil. That is only the beginning of our differences. Joachim is taller than I am. I am heavier than he is. He has three brothers, one more than I have. He likes studying English. He likes studying more than I do. I just want to learn it so that I can study computers. Joachim wants to be an English teacher. Imagine that! _____

_____

Exercise 6. Writing a second draft   Now rewrite your paragraph on a separate piece of paper. Think of a conclusion for your draft paragraph. Add it to your second draft.

D Journal Assignment

Write for ten minutes on each topic. Don't use a dictionary. Don't worry about spelling. Just write.

- Life in my country and life in this country
- My brother (sister) and I
- Comparing myself to my hero
- My language and English
- Myself as a child, myself now

Family and Relationships

A   Prewriting

Exercise 1. Telling the story   Look at the picture story for a few minutes. Think about the story. Next, take turns telling the story. If you hear new words or phrases, write them down next to the following pictures. Ask the person who said the new word or phrase to repeat it and spell it.

1.

2.

3.

4.

Exercise 2. What happened?   Complete the following time line. Follow the picture story. Add your own ideas, too.

PICTURE ONE

First, _____

_____

_____

PICTURE TWO

Next, _____

_____

_____

PICTURE THREE

Then, _____

_____

_____

PICTURE FOUR

Finally, _____

_____

_____

Take turns reading your sentences.

Exercise 3. Word associations from the picture story   The following words could be used to talk about the picture story. Next to each word, write another word that is related to it in some way.

EXAMPLE: coffee (PICTURE ONE)
cup, black, hot, delicious, bitter

baby (PICTURE TWO)
birth, cute, noisy, tiny

1. friend _____

2. married _____

3. doctor _____

4. hospital _____

5. warm _____

6. cold _____

7. holiday _____

8. children _____

 Compare your words with your classmates' words. Write down any new words you learn from them.

```
                        New words




```

 Exercise 4. The qualities of a friend Here are some words to describe people. Think about what qualities are important in a friend. Put the words in order from most important to least important for you.

Important Qualities

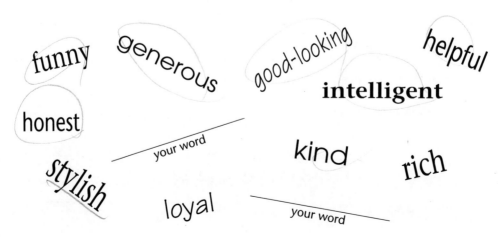

Unit 2: Family and Relationships

23
30

Order of Importance

1. _____   7. _____

2. _____   8. _____

3. _____   9. _____

4. _____   10. _____

5. _____   11. _____

6. _____   12. _____

Exercise 5. Talking about a good friend   Prepare a three-minute talk about a good friend. Use words you have learned in this chapter. Make notes below to help you tell the story. Tell what you like about your good friend. What is special about him or her? Tell a story to show the kind of person your friend is.

After each person speaks, the listeners must ask the speaker a question or make a statement.

EXAMPLE: Where does your friend live now? *or*

You are lucky to have a good friend in this country.

Notes
_____
_____
_____
_____
_____
_____
_____
_____

B   Structure

Exercise 1. Remembering the past   Practice using **used to** + *the simple form of the verb* by changing these sentences from the simple past.

> The two women in the picture story are talking about their college days. They might say something like the following:
>
> We **studied** a lot.
>
> Do you remember you **smoked** like a chimney?
>
> I **wanted** to be a lawyer.
>
> We **went** dancing every Saturday night. It **was** great!
>
> They are talking about what they did regularly in the past. They can also say the following:
>
> We **used to study** a lot.
>
> Do you remember you **used to smoke** like a chimney?
>
> I **used to want** to be a lawyer.
>
> We **used to go** dancing every Saturday night. It **used to be** great!
>
> Use **used to** + *the simple form of the verb* (the one you find in the dictionary) to show an action that happened regularly in the past.

1. I walked to campus every day.

   _____

2. We drank a lot of coffee.

   _____

3. You wore jeans.

   _____

4. We went ice skating a lot.

   _____

Unit 2: Family and Relationships

5. I worked six days a week.

_____

6. You delivered pizza.

_____

7. You were crazy about football.

_____

8. I was a bookworm.

_____

Exercise 2. Talking about your past Think about yourself in high school. What things did you do a lot? Write sentences about these things with **used to** + *the simple form of the verb.*

1. _____

2. _____

3. _____

4. _____

5. _____

Exchange books and read each other's sentences. Did you use to do the same things as your partner?

Exercise 3. English word order Put the following words and phrases into sentences so that the sentences follow English word order. Remember to use a capital letter for the first word in the sentence. Remember to put a period at the end of the sentence.

> In English, the order of the words in a sentence tells us a lot about the meaning of the sentence. The two sentences that follow are different in meaning. In the first sentence, Lucy chases Leona; in the second sentence, Leona chases Lucy.
>
> **EXAMPLE:** My dog, Lucy, used to chase my friend's cat, Leona.
>
> My friend's cat, Leona, used to chase my dog, Lucy.

1. used to talk / we / in the school cafeteria

_____

2. in June / graduated / he / high school

_____

3. she / in the campus bookstore / used to work

_____

4. on Mondays / used to have / a physics class/ I

_____

5. ended/her class / at 5 P.M. / the instructor

_____

6. they / at fast-food restaurants / used to eat dinner

_____

Exercise 4. *Where* and *when* questions   Look at the sentences that you wrote in Exercise 3. Write the prepositional phrases that begin with **at, on,** and **in** in the correct column below.

Where	When

To make questions in the past with **where** and **when,** use the *question word* + **did** + the *simple form of the verb.*

EXAMPLE: We talked in the library.

Where did you talk?

Past form of verbs from Exercise 3	Simple form of verbs from Exercise 3
talked	talk
graduated	graduate
worked	work
had	have
ended	end
ate	eat

Now write questions for the sentences in Exercise 3.

1. _____

2. _____

3. _____

4. _____

5. _____

6. _____

Exercise 5. Asking about the picture story Look at the picture story again. Make questions using the words **when** and **where.** Take turns asking the questions. Use your imagination. Write your questions after you ask them.

1. _____

2. _____

3. _____

4. _____

C Writing and Editing

Exercise 1. Creating a story from key words Use the following words to create a story about the first picture in the picture story. Write your story below the words.

first time

friends   same

laughed   shared

classes   interests

met

Exercise 2. Editing the story   Exchange books with your partner. Use the questions that follow to help your partner improve his or her story. When you are both finished, exchange books again.

1. Are there any words spelled wrong? Write the words correctly.

2. Do all the sentences begin with a capital letter? If not, write the words that need capital letters.

3. Do all the sentences end in a period? If not, put periods after the sentences.

4. Is the story in the past? Are all the verbs used in past form? If not, write the correct past forms of the verbs.

5. Is the word order correct? If not, rewrite the sentence in correct word order.

6. Does the story have a conclusion?

7. Do you understand everything?

8. Do you have any other ideas to help your partner? Write them down.

Exercise 3. Rewriting your paragraph   Rewrite the paragraph from Exercise 2 on a piece of paper. Use your partner's suggestions. Pay attention to the form of your writing. Make sure you use capital letters and periods.

Exercise 4. Talking about meeting a friend   Think of one of your good friends. Try to remember how you met each other. Write down your thoughts here. Use words and phrases. Don't try to write sentences yet.

Notes

_____

_____

_____

_____

_____

_____

_____

_____

Take turns telling about meeting a good friend. After each person speaks, the listeners should each ask a question or make a comment about the story.

Exercise 5. Writing about meeting a friend   Complete the title with your friend's name. Then complete the first sentence. Continue to write the story of your first meeting with your good friend. Remember to tell what happened. What did you say? What did you do? What did your friend say? What did your friend do? Remember to add a concluding sentence at the end.

When I Met _____

I met _____

_____

_____

_____

_____

_____

_____

_____

_____

_____

_____

_____

_____

_____

_____

_____

_____

_____

_____

D Journal Assignment

Write about one of these topics. Write for ten minutes. Don't stop. Don't use a dictionary. Don't worry about spelling or punctuation. Just write.

- My first friend
- A friend for life
- A friend who is like me
- What makes a good friend?
- A friend I used to know

Education

UNIT THREE
CHAPTER 5

A Prewriting

Exercise 1. Writing dialogue   In the following picture story, there are empty spaces for speech. Can you think of what each person says in the story?

1.

1 week later . . .

2.

1 month later . . .

3.

6 months later . . .

4.

What does the teacher say in picture one? Write her words below.

_____

What do the children say in picture two? Write their words below.

_____

What does the boy say in picture three? Write his words below.

_____

What do the children say in picture four? Write their words below.

_____

 Now read your classmate's sentences. Do you have the same ideas? Decide what you both want to write for each bubble in the story. The two of you should write the same story here.

PICTURE ONE _____

_____

PICTURE TWO _____

_____

PICTURE THREE _____

_____

PICTURE FOUR _____

_____

Compare your story with the story of two other classmates. First, read your story to them. Then, listen to their story.

Exercise 2. Finding words in the picture story The following words can be found in the picture story on page 46. Write each word near the object in one of the pictures.

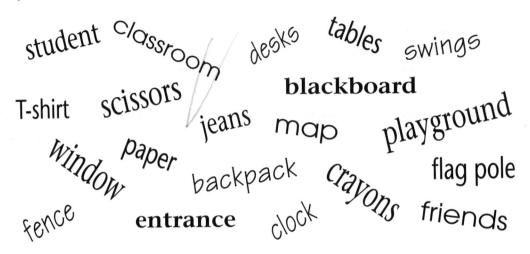

student classroom desks tables swings

T-shirt scissors blackboard

jeans map playground

window paper backpack crayons flag pole

fence entrance clock friends

Exercise 3. Talking about your primary school classroom Think about when you were 8 or 9 years old. What was the name of your school? Where was it? Use some of the words from Exercise 2 to talk about your classroom, your school, and your classmates. Make some notes before you speak. The notes will help you remember what to say.

EXAMPLE: village school, pretty teacher, crowded classroom

Notes

_____

_____

_____

_____

_____

_____

_____

Unit 3: Education

Exercise 4. Telling the picture story   Look at the picture story on page 46. Each person in the group will talk about one picture in the story. Together you will tell the story of the little boy. Begin with these words: *In this picture, the little boy . . .* Practice telling the story in your group. Then join another group. First, one group tells the story. Then, the other tells the story. Finally, listen to the teacher tell the story.

Exercise 5. Comparing the story to experience   Think about the picture story on page 46. Think about your own primary school experience. If something was the same, you can write that it was the same. If something was different, you can write that it was different.

> **EXAMPLE:**   My classroom was **like** the classroom in the story. It had desks and chairs.
>
> My teacher was **different from** the teacher in the story. My teacher was an old man.

Now write five sentences that compare your experience to the story.

1. _____

2. _____

3. _____

4. _____

5. _____

B   Structure

Exercise 1. Using direct speech   Rewrite the following sentences into direct speech. Follow the rules for punctuation and capitalization.

> **EXAMPLE:**   The teacher said you are a good student.
> The teacher said, "You are a good student."

Direct Speech

When we write exactly what people say, we write direct speech.

EXAMPLE: The teacher said, "You are a good student."

It is most common to begin with the speaker.

EXAMPLE: The teacher

Next, use a verb of speaking. If the speech is finished, use a past tense form.

EXAMPLES: The teacher said, . . .

The teacher shouted, . . .

The teacher cried, . . .

- Use a comma (,) to separate the speaker and the verb from the quotation.
- Use quotation marks (". . .") around the words of the speaker.
- Use a capital letter at the beginning of the quotation.
- Put the period or question mark inside the final quotation mark.

1. The teacher said Juanita is going to New York.

_____

2. Ivan said my wife is studying English.

_____

3. Lyubov said the children do not have their book bags.

_____

4. Mohammad said it is time for a break.

_____

5. The instructor asked does anyone know the answer?

_____

Exercise 2. Remembering what your teacher used to say Think about your primary school teacher. What are some things he or she used to say to you and your classmates? Remember to use quotation marks.

EXAMPLES: My fourth grade teacher used to shout, "Class, please be quiet!"

Mr. Kitano always said, "No chewing gum in class!"

1. _____

2. _____

3. _____

4. _____

5. _____

Imagine that the other students in the group are your class. You are your primary school teacher. Try to speak as he or she did. Stand up. Walk as your teacher walked. Do what your teacher did. Say the sentences you wrote. Your "students" can answer you if they want to. When you listen to the other "teachers and students," try to write down what they say.

_____ said, _____
(name)

_____

_____

_____

_____

Exercise 3. Using *say* and *tell* in indirect speech   Choose **say** or **tell**. Write the verb in the past (**said, told**).

EXAMPLE: The student _____told_____ the teacher that he was sick.

Indirect Speech

When you do not write a person's exact words, you do not use quotation marks or a capital letter. This is called **indirect speech.**

EXAMPLE: *Direct speech:*   The teacher said, "You got an A on the test."
   Indirect speech: The teacher said I got an A on the test.

Notice that **you** changes to **I** in indirect speech. If you include both the speaker and the person *spoken to,* use the verb **tell.**

EXAMPLE: **The teacher** told **me** I got an A on the test.

---

1. The principal _____ to respect our school.

2. The principal _____ us to respect our school.

3. The teacher _____ we should always come to class on time.

4. The students _____ they had too much homework.

5. The teacher _____ me to always do my best.

6. My parents _____ me that an education was important for my future.

7. The instructor _____ the class to prepare for the exam.

8. My mother _____ it is always important to be honest.

C Writing and Editing

Exercise 1. Writing out the picture story You have practiced speaking and writing about the story on page 46. Now write the story below. Write two sentences for each picture. One of the sentences must contain direct or indirect speech **(say/said, tell/told).**

PICTURE ONE _____

_____

PICTURE TWO _____

_____

PICTURE THREE _____

_____

PICTURE FOUR _____

_____

Exercise 2. Writing linking sentences The story is about one boy. Each of the pictures shows something different. Go back to Exercise 1. Write in time expressions at the beginning of some sentences to link the picture story. Give the boy a name. Add a title for your story. Recopy it all on the next page.

Use expressions of time at the beginning of a sentence to create links in a story. These expressions are separated from the rest of the sentence by a comma. Time expressions are boldfaced in the examples that follow.

EXAMPLES: **For the first few weeks,** he didn't speak much, but he watched and listened.

In a few months, his English improved a lot.

One day, he spoke in front of the class.

_____

(title)

_____
_____
_____
_____
_____
_____
_____
_____
_____
_____

Exercise 3. Free writing   Think of your first day in primary school. Can you remember how it was? What did you think of your school? your teacher? your classmates? What did you do on that first day? Did anything special happen? Did you eat anything at school? What time did you go home? What did you do after school that day?

Now you are ready to start free writing about your first day of primary school. Free writing means writing as thoughts come into your mind. Don't worry about grammar, spelling, or form. Don't erase. Don't use a dictionary. Give yourself freedom to write. Write for ten minutes without stopping.

Memories of My First Day in Primary School

_____
_____
_____
_____
_____

_____

_____

_____

_____

_____

_____

_____

_____

_____

_____

_____

_____

_____

_____

_____

 Read your free writing to your partner.

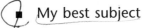

feel peaceful
peaceful

D Journal Assignment

Pick one of these ideas. Write for ten minutes. Write in a quiet and comfortable place. Write when you feel peaceful.

月水金

- My first school friend
- The perfect primary school
- The best thing my teacher ever told me
- My best subject
- The worst thing about my primary school

Education

A **Prewriting**

Exercise 1. Good story/bad story Look at the following picture story. Name all the things you see. Write the words next to the pictures. First, one person tells a *good* story about the boy and his education. Use your imagination. Then the other person tells a *bad* story about the boy and his education.

1.

2.

3.

4.

Exercise 2. Finding partners   Look at the words you wrote down next to the picture story. Write twelve of those words under Column A.

Column A	Column B
1. _____	_____
2. _____	_____
3. _____	_____
4. _____	_____
5. _____	_____
6. _____	_____
7. _____	_____
8. _____	_____
9. _____	_____
10. _____	_____
11. _____	_____
12. _____	_____

Now in Column B, write a related word for each word in Column A. You can write a synonym (a word with the same meaning), an antonym (a word with the opposite meaning), or a word that simply goes with the first one.

EXAMPLES: boy

synonym   guy

antonym   girl

related word   man

 Exercise 3. Comparing pictures   Look at the picture story on page 56 again. Choose pictures 1 and 4 or 2 and 3. Look closely. What is similar in both pictures? What is different? You and your partner make notes on the next page.

Similarities	**Differences**
_____	_____
_____	_____
_____	_____
_____	_____
_____	_____
_____	_____
_____	_____
_____	_____

Exercise 4. Creating a group story   Find two more people for your group. Tell a story about the pictures. Each person takes one picture to talk about. Use your notes from Exercise 3.

Exercise 5. Group dictation   One group will tell its story to the other group. Each person will tell his or her part of the story. The first time, just listen to the story. Then, listen a second time. This time, stop the story teller if you do not understand him or her. Ask about new words. Now you are ready for dictation. The story tellers will tell their story two more times. You will write their story below.

Now read the story that you wrote again. Add a title for the story.

B Structure

Exercise 1. *Better* and *the best* Look at the phrases that follow. Write one sentence with **good.** Write another sentence with **better.** Write a third sentence with **best.** Write your opinion.

	In one person's opinion
Some things are good.	Listening to a CD is **good.**
Some things are better.	Attending a concert is **better than** listening to a CD.
Some things are the best.	Making your own music is **the best.**

1. cooking for yourself / eating at a restaurant / going to a friend's house for dinner

   _____

   _____

   _____

2. watching basketball on TV / going to a basketball game / playing basketball

   _____

   _____

   _____

3. learning from others / studying in school / teaching yourself

   _____

   _____

   _____

4. learning with computers / learning through books / learning from videos

   _____

   _____

   _____

5. Put your own words here. Then write three sentences.

_____ / _____ / _____

_____

_____

_____

Exercise 2. The best things Give your opinion about the ideas below.
Write **I agree** or **I disagree.**

EXAMPLE: Charlie Chaplin was the best comedian who ever made a movie.

I agree. I think Charlie Chaplin was the best comedian who ever
made a movie. *or*

I disagree. I think Roberto Benigni is the best comedian who ever
made a movie.

Agree or disagree?

Your own experience is *the best* teacher.

_____

_____

Do you agree with the preceding statement? If you do, copy the sentence after
I agree. I think . . .

I agree. I think _____

Do you disagree with the preceding statement? If you disagree, write your idea
after **I disagree. I think . . .**

I disagree. I think _____

1. Jackie Chan is the best action hero.

_____

2. Men are the best world leaders.

_____

3. Computer technology is the best educational tool.

_____

4. Studying with a master is the best way to learn.

_____

5. Reading is the best way for an adult to learn a new language.

_____

6. Public education is the best education.

_____

7. Write your idea here.

_____

Exercise 3. Comparing your ideas of the best things with those of your classmates   Read your sentences from Exercise 2 to compare your ideas with those of your classmates. Talk about why you agree or disagree with each other.

Exercise 4. *Worse* **and** *the worst*   Look at the phrases that follow. Write one sentence with **bad.** Write another sentence with **worse.** Write a third sentence with **the worst.**

	In one person's opinion
Some things are bad.	Getting a D on a test is **bad.**
Some things are worse.	Getting an F on a test is **worse.**
Some things are the worst.	Getting an F in a course is **the worst.**

1. losing an assignment / losing your book bag / losing your wallet

_____

_____

_____

2. going to class on a beautiful day / going to class with a headache / going to class with a cold

_____

_____

_____

3. taking a test on your birthday / taking a quiz when you didn't study / taking a final exam when you are sick

_____

_____

_____

4. cheating on a test / copying another student's homework / sleeping in class

_____

_____

_____

5. being illiterate / cutting classes / dropping out of school

_____

_____

_____

Exercise 5. The worst things Give your opinion about the following ideas. Remember to first write **I agree** or **I disagree.**

Agree or disagree?

Lack of education is **the worst** problem for most poor people.

_____

_____

Do you agree with the preceding statement? If you do, copy the sentence after **I agree. In my opinion, . . .**

I agree. In my opinion, _____

Do you disagree with the preceding statement? If you do, write your idea after **I disagree. In my opinion, . . .**

I disagree. In my opinion, _____

1. Poor health is the worst problem for young schoolchildren.

   _____

2. An unfair teacher is the worst kind of teacher.

   _____

3. Lack of computers is the worst problem for many schools.

   _____

4. Lack of money for education is the worst problem that most people have.

   _____

5. Expensive textbooks are the worst problem for students.

   _____

6. Lack of educational opportunity is the worst problem for poor people.

   _____

7. Write your idea.

   _____

 Exercise 6. Comparing your ideas of the worst things with those of your classmates Read your sentences to compare your ideas with those of your classmates. Talk about why you agree or disagree with each other.

C Writing and Editing

Exercise 1. Freewriting—a perfect school   Close your eyes and relax. Think of a school. It is the perfect school. It is the best school in the world. What does it look like? Who teaches there? Who studies there? What subjects do the students study?

Now open your eyes. Write for ten minutes about a perfect school. Write about the one that you saw in your mind. Keep writing. Don't stop until the instructor says to stop. Don't worry about spelling, grammar, or punctuation. Just write.

A   Perfect   School

_____

_____

_____

_____

_____

_____

_____

_____

_____

_____

_____

_____

_____

_____

_____

_____

_____

_____

_____

Exchange your writing with your partner. Write two positive comments on your partner's paper. Begin with "I like . . ."

_____

_____

Exercise 2. Editing for capital letters   Edit this passage for capital letters. Circle all the letters that should be capitalized.

Remember these capitalization rules.

■ Use a capital letter if the word is part of a specific name, title, or place.
   EXAMPLE: John, Doctor Smith, New Haven

■ Use a capital letter if the word is the name of a language, people, or country.
   EXAMPLE: French, Mexicans, Finland

■ Use a capital letter at the beginning of a quotation.
   EXAMPLE: Joanne said, "Don't leave without me."

---

myung hee went to a small elementary school in hallim, a village on the southwest side of cheju island. when she was twelve, she entered girl's central middle school in a nearby city. her english instructor, mr. kang, said that she had a good ear for languages. her english got better through high school in seoul, the capital city of the republic of korea. myung hee attended ewha women's university and graduated with honors in english. after graduation she went to australia to study more. at first she was disappointed because she could not understand australians when they spoke. eventually her english improved. people would say, "you're australian, aren't you?" when myung hee would say no, people would say, "but you sound like you're from australia!"

Exercise 3. Preparing an educational autobiography Think about your education and complete the following chart.

School name	City or town	Years attended	Names of one or two teachers	Anything special that happened

Write down your feelings about your education. Did you like to go to school? Were you confident?

_____

_____

_____

_____

 Discuss your educational autobiography with your partner.

Exercise 4. Writing your educational autobiography Use the information from Exercise 3 to write a paragraph about your education. Use words like **first, next, then** and **after that** to connect your ideas.

_____

_____

_____

_____

_____

_____

_____

_____

_____

_____

_____

_____

_____

_____

_____

_____

Exercise 5. Group editing Pass your paragraph around the group. Attach a blank piece of paper to it. Write two questions to each group member about his or her paragraph. The questions should be about other information you want to know. When you get your paragraph and paper back, there should be six questions on the paper. Write an answer to each one. Next, decide if you want to include the information from your classmates' questions in your paragraph.

Exercise 6. Rewriting your paragraph   Rewrite your paragraph. Include at least three new sentences from Exercise 5.

Read your paragraph to your group. Ask your group mates if the paragraph sounds better with the new information. If it does, check your paragraph for spelling and capital letters. Then hand it in to your instructor. If it doesn't, ask the group for ideas to make it better. Then include those ideas. Finally, follow the step above to check for spelling and capital letters before you hand the paragraph in to your instructor.

Unit 3: Education

D Journal Assignment

Pick one of these ideas. Write when you feel relaxed and you are in a quiet place. Take five minutes to think about the topic before you write. Then write for ten minutes.

- Education in my country
- The best teacher
- What should we teach children?
- Public education, private education
- How much is a good education worth?
- Something I taught myself

UNIT FOUR

CHAPTER 7

Work

A Prewriting

Exercise 1. Using a word list   Use the word list on page 71 to talk about the picture story. You must use at least one word from the list in each sentence you make. You can change the word.

EXAMPLES: singular to plural for nouns   **worker → workers**

tense change for verbs   **works → worked**

1.

2.

3.

4.

work	job	hard	alone	pay
raise	laborer	injury	muscles	boss
drinking	bartender	waste	money	needs
promotion	difficult	drive	stack	hours

Exercise 2. Creating a character   Look closely at the picture story on page 70 again. Take ten minutes to prepare a story about the pictures. The following questions will help you prepare. Make notes next to each question.

1. Who is this person? _____

2. What is his name? _____

3. Where does he live? _____

4. Whom does he live with? _____

5. What are two words that describe his character? _____

6. How did he get his job? _____

7. Why does he do this work? _____

8. What does he want from life? _____

9. What does he think of his life? _____

10. What does he think about his future? _____

Exercise 3. Paired dictation   Tell your partner the story you created in Exercise 1. Tell it slowly so your partner can write it down. When you have finished telling your story, your partner will tell you his or her story. Write your partner's story below.

_____

_____

_____

_____

_____

_____

_____

_____

_____

_____

Exercise 4. Brainstorming   Put a blank piece of paper in the middle of your group. Write the words _hard work_ in the middle of the paper. Each person should write words and phrases on the paper. Write whatever you think when you see the words _hard work._ Fill the paper with words.

    EXAMPLE: hard work: my mother, money, . . .

Exercise 5. Writing from a brainstorming session   Copy the words from Exercise 4 into your notebook. Use at least ten of these words and phrases in a paragraph. Write about _hard work_ on page 73. Write whatever comes to mind about this topic. Write freely. Don't worry about grammar and spelling now.

```
                        H a r d    W o r k


    _____

    _____

    _____

    _____

    _____

    _____

    _____

    _____

    _____

    _____
```

 Now read your paragraph to your group. Try to put some feeling or emotion into your reading.

B Structure

 Exercise 1. How long has he been working there?   In the first picture, the young man is working in a warehouse. In the second picture, he is still working in the same place. How much time has passed between the two pictures. A month? A year? A few years? Several years?

How long has he been working there?

He has been working there for _____.

Use the present perfect progressive tense to show an action that began in the past and continues into the present. The **-ing** emphasizes a continuing action.

Use **have/has** + **been** + *verb* + **ing.**

   EXAMPLE: I have been speaking English since I came to this country.

Now look at picture 3. Where is the man? What is he doing? Imagine that you are interviewing him. Ask him a question like the one above. Write the question below.

_____

_____

Now look at picture 4. What could you ask the man? Write the question below.

_____

_____

Exercise 2. What have we been doing? Circle the activities that you have been doing since you came to this country.

studying English	cooking for yourself	driving to school
working full-time	working part-time	living alone
supporting yourself	speaking two languages	watching TV
feeling homesick	meeting new people	writing in a journal

Exchange books with your partner. Look at the activities that he or she circled. Ask a question for each activity circled. Write the answers down on a piece of paper.

EXAMPLE: How long have you been working full-time?

Exercise 3. Writing about your classmate Write five interesting questions to ask your partner. (You will write the answers later.)

1. _____?

(answer) _____

2. _____?

(answer) _____

3. _____?

(answer) _____

4. _____ ?

(answer) _____

5. _____ ?

(answer) _____

Now ask your questions and write your partner's answers. Write short answers. Then answer your partner's questions.

EXAMPLE: How long have you been playing soccer?
Since I was 8 years old.

How long have you been wearing your hair like that?
For six months.

Use **since** to show a point in time when an activity or situation began. Use **for** to show the period of time that an activity or situation has been in existence.

EXAMPLE:

since	for
1990	10 years
9 A.M. this morning	a couple of hours
I was 6 years old	fifteen years

Now, write sentences about your partner with the information that you have. Begin the first sentence with your partner's name. Begin the other sentences with **he** or **she**.

_____

_____

_____

_____

_____

_____

Exercise 4. Talking about yourself Write sentences about yourself using **for** and **since.** Follow the outline below.

EXAMPLE: I've* been working as a chef for two years.

1. I've been _____ for _____.

2. I've been _____ since _____.

3. I've been _____ for _____.

4. I've been _____ since _____.

Read around the group, one person and one sentence at a time. Try to read sentences that are like the ones you hear. Ask questions about what your classmates say.

*I've = I have

C Writing and Editing

Exercise 1. Organizing to write Think about the first job you had. Think about your boss. Think about your work conditions. Think about your feelings.

Here is an example of the first job of one of the authors of this text. When he was young, a typical job for a young boy was to deliver newspapers around the neighborhood. Part of the job was to collect money for the newspapers each week. Usually people gave the paper boy a tip. Now in North America, adults deliver newspapers early in the morning and the company sends the bill to the customers.

Lou's First Job

About me	About my boss	About my work conditions	About my feelings
• 12 years old • didn't know about work • wanted money • friends were doing it	• wore a white shirt and tie every day • had dark hair • was always busy • never talked to me	• picked up newspapers at a small store • folded papers and put them in bag on my bike • rode to my route • started after school • tried to finish before dark	• worried about dogs • got mad at people who weren't home when I collected • got mad when I didn't get a tip • felt good when I had no more papers to deliver

Now put your information in the chart that follows. If you have never had a job, write about someone in your family.

My First Job

About me	About my boss	About my work conditions	About my feelings

Exercise 2. Talking through your experience Each person in your group takes a turn to tell about his or her first job. Make notes about words, ideas, and experiences that you want to know more about.

Notes

After a person tells a story, ask questions.

Exercise 3. Writing about your first job Reread your chart. Is there anything else to add? Add it. Think of a few words or phrases to describe your first job.

My First Job

Do these words really express your feelings about this first job? These words are the focus of your writing. This means that the feeling a reader gets when he or she reads your paragraph is contained in these words. Write a paragraph about your first job on page 79. Be sure to keep your focus. You do not need to include all of the information from your chart.

Exercise 4. Community editing Put your paragraph about your first job on your desk. Put a blank sheet of paper next to it. Get out of your seat. Go to another desk. Read the paragraph.

Write down the following: your opinion of the story

ideas for improving the story

words or phrases you like

any spelling or grammar corrections

Read and comment about as many paragraphs as you can. When the teacher calls time, return to your desk. Read what your classmates have written. Decide what to change in your story.

Exercise 5. Rewriting Rewrite your story on a piece of paper. Make any changes that you want. Hand it in to your teacher.

D Journal Assignment

Choose a different topic for each day of the week. Each day write about each one for ten minutes. Don't stop. At the end of the week, read all that you have written. What do the journal entries tell you?

- The good boss
- Working alone, working with others
- Kid's work
- A job I wouldn't do
- What is good work?
- My own boss
- A bad job

Work

A Prewriting

Exercise 1. Recalling information   Think about the man in the story in Chapter 7. What can you remember about him and his working life? Write what you remember below.

_____

_____

_____

Each person in your group will take a turn telling what he or she remembers.

Exercise 2. What has happened?   Think about the man in the picture story on page 83. What has happened to him? Why is he being interviewed? Write six questions to ask the man.

1. _____

2. _____

3. _____

4. _____

5. _____

6. _____

One person plays the man in the picture story. The other person is the job interviewer. The job interviewer asks the man questions. Change roles after asking the six questions.

Exercise 3. Creating a work history Look at the picture story. Imagine that you are that man. Write a question in the speech bubble in picture 2. Tell the story from the point of view of the man. Talk about what you used to do and what you have done.

used to - what you did in the past, but not now

have done - past experience that is important now

Write down some important points of your work experience here.

_____

_____

Each person in your group will talk for two minutes. You will take the role of the man. You will speak in the first person: **I.**

Exercise 4. Creating a resume Create a resume, a written record with personal information, education, specialized training, and work history for the man in the picture story. Use your imagination to fill in the missing information in the following chart.

First name and last name	
Street address	
City, state, zip code	
Telephone number	
Email address (optional)	
Education	
Specialized training	
Work history (name of company, job title, job description, dates; begin with present job)	

Exercise 5. Talking about different kinds of work The man in the picture stories in Chapter 7 and Chapter 8 started out doing physical labor—using his strength to do work. Later he moved to a job that did not require using strength. Think about the jobs that people do. Write the name of a job in one of the categories in the following chart. Try to write at least ten different jobs.

Physical work (requires strength or hand skills)	Mental work (requires long periods of thinking and planning)	Service work (requires serving others or helping others)
construction worker	mathematician	flight attendant

Compare your list with your partner's list. Explain to your partner why you put each job in one of the categories. Add new jobs to your list as you learn about them.

B Structure

Exercise 1. Ordering events in the two stories Read the following list of activities. In our story, some events happened before other events. Connect the events from the First Column to the events in the Then Column by drawing a line from one to the other.

First	**Then**
1. stacked boxes in a warehouse	a. sold forklifts
2. worked all day long	b. got the job
3. worked as a forklift driver	c. went for a drink at a bar
4. went for a job interview	d. drove a forklift
5. drove forklifts	e. worked as a salesman

Now write a sentence for each pair of connected events. Use the words **first** and **then.** Be sure to use a comma before **and.**

> EXAMPLE: First, he worked near his home, and then he found a job far away from home.

1. _____

2. _____

3. _____

4. _____

5. _____

Exercise 2. Using *before* to link two events   Another way to show the relationship between two events is to use **before.**

> Use **before** with the second event of two events. For variety in your writing, use the gerund form of the verb (*verb* + **ing**) with **before.**
>
> > EXAMPLE: He worked near his home before finding a job far away. *or*
> >
> > He worked near his home before he found a job far away.
>
> You can also put the clause that begins with **before** at the front of the sentence.
>
> > EXAMPLE: Before finding a job far away from home, he worked near his home.

Rewrite the sentences in Exercise 1 using **before** + *gerund.*

1. _____

2. _____

3. _____

4. _____

5. _____

Exercise 3. Discussing work history Use the resume in Part A, Exercise 4. Talk about the man's work history. Use **before** + *gerund.* Make notes for your discussion below.

Notes

_____

_____

_____

_____

_____

_____

_____

Exercise 4. Using *after* to link two events Another way to show the relationship between two events is to use **after.**

Use **after** with the first event of two events. For variety in your writing, use the gerund form of the verb (*verb* + **ing**) with **after.**

EXAMPLE: He found a job far away from home after working near his home.

or

He found a job far away from home after he worked near his home.

You can also put the part of the sentence that begins with **after** at the front of the sentence.

EXAMPLE: After working near his home, he found a job far away from home.

Change the sentences in Exercise 2 to sentences with **after** + *gerund.*

1. _____

2. _____

3. _____

4. _____

5. _____

 Exercise 5. Making a short speech about your work experience Prepare a 3-minute speech about your work experience. You will give your speech to your classmates. Make some notes below to organize your experience in time order. If you do not have work experience, then write about a friend or family member who does. Begin your notes with your most recent experience.

Job and duties	Name of company and location	Month and year started to month and year ended job	How you felt about your job	Other information

Unit 4: Work

Practice your speech at home. You can begin with your first job or with your current job. Use **then, after,** and **before** in your speech. Remember to include details to keep your speech interesting to your listeners.

When you speak, use your notes, but do not read them and do not look down at them. After you listen to a classmate's speech, write a question to the speaker about what he or she said.

C Writing and Editing

Exercise 1. Quick write on what a teacher does   Think of teachers you have known. Think about what they do. Write for ten minutes on this topic: "What a teacher does." Don't worry about spelling, grammar, or style. Just write. Try to fill up a whole page in your notebook.

Exercise 2. Explaining a job   Think of a job that you have done or a job you know about.

Write the name of the job here _____

EXAMPLE: chef

Think of how that job fits into the industry or profession of which it is a part.

Write the name of the industry or profession here _____

EXAMPLE: hotel and restaurant industry

Now think about what a person does in that job. Write what the person does below.

_____

EXAMPLE: prepares food and creates dishes

What is your opinion of the job's importance? Write why the job is important or not important below.

_____

EXAMPLE: Good food is important.

Explain to your group what job you chose. Tell your group about it. Ask your group mates if they have any questions about the job. Answer their questions. Make notes below about any additional information you want to add.

Notes

_____

_____

_____

_____

_____

_____

_____

Exercise 3. Partner Swap* Swap books. Use your partner's information from Exercise 2 to write a paragraph on a piece of writing paper. When you finish, give your partner back his or her book. Give your partner the paragraph that you wrote.

*Swap means change or exchange.

Exercise 4. Rewriting the paragraph Use your own information and your partner's paragraph to rewrite the paragraph on a piece of paper.

Exercise 5. Comparing paragraphs and giving feedback With a new partner, exchange the paragraphs you wrote in Exercises 3 and 4. Ask your new partner to write comments about the differences in the two paragraphs.

Comments

_____

_____

_____

_____

_____

_____

_____

Read the comments and reread the paragraphs. Think about any changes you want to make. Write a second draft of your paragraph from Exercise 4. Make changes and corrections.

D Journal Assignment

Choose one topic from the following list. Write each day for ten minutes about that topic.

- What I want to do
- My father's work
- Unemployed
- Follow your heart to your job
- Make money, be happy
- Working for others

Leisure and Recreation

A Prewriting

Exercise 1. Brainstorming   Think of as many words as you can that relate to the picture and its title.

The Basketball Game

The Fan

The Concert

Congratulations

My group's words

_____

_____

_____

_____

Exercise 2. A basketball player and a cellist In the picture story, the woman is a basketball player. The man is a cellist.

Do you know the names of popular team sports?

Do you know the positions in each sport?

Do you know the names of common musical instruments?

Do you know the names for people who play these instruments?

Try to complete the following chart. Add information about other sports or instruments.

Sport	Positions	Instrument	Musician
basketball	center (4 others)	cello	cellist
baseball	(9)	piano	
	goalie (10 others)		drummer

(Continued)

Sport	Positions	Instrument	Musician
volleyball	(6)	trumpet	
	quarterback (10 others)		violinist
rugby	hooker (14 others)	flute	flutist
water polo	goalie (5 others)	guitar	guitarist

Exercise 3. Talking about sports and music   One partner chooses sports. The other chooses music. Use the following words to talk about your topic with your partner. Talk together for at least five minutes.

	Sports	
play	practice	position
compete	win	lose
kick	run	throw

	Music	
play	listen	practice
dance	kind of music	
band	perform	instrument

Unit 5: Leisure and Recreation

Exercise 4. Telling the story   Make up a story about the people in the pictures. Give names to the female basketball player and the male cellist. Give the woman's basketball team a name. Think about the relationship between the woman and the man. Include all of this in your story. Make notes below to prepare in telling the story. Then tell the story to your partner.

Notes

_____

_____

_____

_____

_____

_____

_____

_____

Exercise 5. Asking questions for more information   After you listen to your partner's story, prepare questions. What more do you want to know about the woman and the man? Use at least three of the question words that follow.

Who?   What?   When?

Where?   Why?

How much?   How many?

1. _____

2. _____

3. _____

4. _____

5. _____

B Structure

Exercise 1. Where do you go to enjoy yourself?   Where do you go to enjoy yourself? **To** a movie? **To** the beach? **To** a concert? Write five sentences about where you go to enjoy yourself.

1. _____
2. _____
3. _____
4. _____
5. _____

Swap books with a partner. Read each other's sentences. Do you do the same things or different things to enjoy yourself?

Exercise 2. Where is everything?   In a city or town, there is usually an entertainment area, a place where there are *theaters* and *clubs.* There is usually a *large stadium* or *building for sports* somewhere, too. There is also a place to go *shopping*, perhaps a *shopping mall.*

Use some of the words that follow to describe where facilities are located in your hometown or in this town or city.

downtown   on the outskirts of the city (town)   uptown
on the west side   in the center of   on the east side
next to   near   across from
on the north side   far from   on the south side

EXAMPLES: There is a shopping mall near the bus station.

There is a theater downtown.

1. _____
2. _____
3. _____
4. _____
5. _____

Exercise 3. *At, in,* or *on*? Where do you do it? Complete the sentences with **at, in,** or **on.** There are two choices for each sentence.

- Use **at, in,** or **on** to locate things or activities in places.
- Use **at** to show that something or someone is present in, at, or near something else

    EXAMPLE: I swim at Los Banos Pool.

- Use **on** to show that something is in contact with the top surface of something else

    EXAMPLES: The runners are racing on the track.

    Dan is sailing on his boat.

- Use **in** for inside buildings or specific areas.

    EXAMPLE: in the concert hall

---

1. You can see that movie _____ (on, at) the Cineplex Five.

2. The camping is good _____ (on, in) Mt. Shasta.

3. Bears live _____ (on, in) Yosemite Park.

4. I like playing _____ (on, in) these tennis courts.

5. Supong is swimming laps _____ (on, in) the pool.

6. That's Hector _____ (on, in) the soccer field.

7. Pavel has played ice hockey _____ (on, at) the Molson Center.

8. Juha and Sami are supposed to meet us _____ (on, at) the concert.

9. The tournament is played _____ (on, at) Wimbledon.

10. There's only one piece left _____ (on, at) the chessboard.

Exercise 4. What do you do for fun?   Use the following words to write five sentences about what you do for fun. Add details to explain *with whom* or *where.*

EXAMPLE: I like to go golfing with my friends.

I like to play golf at Great Hills Lake.

read	**go:**
play	shopping
watch	fishing
listen to	golfing
practice	mountain climbing
	hiking
	dancing
	jogging
	swimming

1. _____

2. _____

3. _____

4. _____

5. _____

Exercise 5. When are you doing it?   Write sentences telling about the next time you are doing each activity. Use **at, on,** or **in.**

EXAMPLE: I'm going fishing on Saturday.

- Use **at, on,** and **in** with time expressions.
- Use **at** with a specific time.
    EXAMPLE: I'm going to play tennis at 5 o'clock.
- Use **on** with a day of the week.
    EXAMPLE: I'm going to play soccer on Sunday.
- Use **in** with a period of time.
    EXAMPLE: I'm going to go skiing in two weeks.

Unit 5: Leisure and Recreation

1. _____

2. _____

3. _____

4. _____

5. _____

C Writing and Editing

Exercise 1. What do they have to do?   In the picture story, there is a basketball player and a cellist. Each one of them has to practice. List the things that they need to practice in the following chart.

Basketball player	Cellist
practice shooting	practice scales

Exercise 2. How to become a good basketball player/how to become a good cellist Use the information in Exercise 1 to write a paragraph about a basketball player or a cellist. Choose one of these sentences for your introduction.

1. To become a good _____, you have to do several things.

2. There are _____ things you must do to become a good _____.

3. What does it take to become a good _____?

Now write your paragraph below.

Becoming a Good _____

_____

_____

_____

_____

_____

_____

_____

_____

_____

_____

_____

_____

Exercise 3. Editing in an expert group Find two students who have written about the same or similar topic. Read each other's paragraphs. Help the other students with grammar, spelling, and style, if you can.

Make notes about what you like in the other students' paragraphs or write down new ideas to include in your paragraph.

Notes

_____

_____

_____

_____

_____

_____

_____

_____

Exercise 4. Rewriting the second draft Use the information you got in Exercise 2 to rewrite your own paragraph.

Becoming a Good _____

_____

_____

_____

_____

_____

_____

_____

_____

_____

_____

_____

_____

Exercise 5. Copying the expert, yourself   Think about something that you do well. Write what it is here: _____.

What do you have to do to be good at it? Make notes below.

Notes

_____

_____

_____

_____

_____

_____

_____

_____

Now use the paragraph that you wrote in Exercise 4 as a model. Write a paragraph about what you do well.

Becoming a Good _____

_____

_____

_____

_____

_____

_____

_____

_____

_____

_____

_____

_____

_____

Read your paragraph to the group. Read it slowly and clearly so that everyone can understand you. Ask your group mates if they want to know anything more. Make notes in your paragraph. Rewrite your paragraph on a blank sheet of paper. Hand it in to your teacher.

D Journal Assignment

Choose two 10-minute topics for the first two journal writing days. Choose two 15-minute topics for the next two journal writing days.

- How to score a goal in soccer (10)
- How to make a dress (or any other article of clothing) (10)
- A game I won (15)
- A game I lost (15)
- At the movies (10)
- At a rock concert (or any kind of musical concert) (10)
- How to play guitar (you can put any instrument in place of guitar) (15)
- How to shop cheaply (15)
- The world's best athlete (10)
- The worst team I have ever seen (10)
- Playing cards for money (15)
- Chess and checkers (15)

Leisure and Recreation

A Prewriting

Exercise 1. It's good to have time for each other   Look at the picture story. You see that the two women are friends. They have grown up together. They have shared time together. They enjoy each other.

1.

2.

3.

4.

1. Do you have a close friend? _____

2. Do you enjoy being with your friend? _____

3. If you have a close friend, write down his or her name. _____

4. How long have you known her or him? _____

5. What do you do together? _____

6. Do you enjoy being alone? _____

7. When do you like to be alone? _____

8. When you are alone, what do you do? _____

9. Where do you go alone? _____

Tell your partner about your close friend and about when you are alone.

Exercise 2. Comparing leisure activities   In the picture story, the two women have shared time with each other since they were little girls. On the other hand, their activities have changed. Write down what activity they are doing in each picture.

PICTURE ONE _____

_____

PICTURE TWO _____

_____

PICTURE THREE _____

_____

PICTURE FOUR _____

_____

Think about how you have spent your time since you were young. Compare your activities with the activities of the women.

EXAMPLE: The little girls played with dolls, but when I was little, I played soccer.

Exchange stories with your partner. Make notes about what your partner says.

Notes

 Exercise 3. Moving around, sitting down   In picture 1, the girls are sitting down and having tea with their dolls. In picture 2, the girls are playing soccer. They are moving around. In your group, make a list of activities that you do sitting down and a list of activities that you do moving around.

Activity list

Sitting down	Moving around

Exercise 4. Which doesn't belong? The girls are playing with dolls in picture 1. They are chatting over coffee in picture 4. These two activities have some similarities. They are social. They are not competitive.

The girls are playing soccer in picture 2. They are jogging in picture 3. These two activities have some similarities. They require energy. Speed is important. These activities can be competitive.

Look at the groups of activities below. Underline the word in each group that does not belong. In your group, take turns telling each other what each group of words has in common. Also tell which word does not belong with the others.

EXAMPLE: reading / writing poetry / watching movies / <u>playing soccer</u>

I underlined playing soccer because it is a sport and you play on a team. Reading, writing poetry, and watching movies are not sports. You can do them alone, too.

1. baseball / football / basketball / horseback riding

2. slot machines / roulette / chess / poker

3. bull riding / calf roping / swimming / hunting

4. ice hockey / skiing / surfing / skating

5. shopping / going to garage sales / window shopping / watching TV

6. auto racing / going to a dog show / bike racing / horse racing

7. stamp collecting / antique shopping / art collecting / making pottery

8. sky diving / hang gliding / bowling / skateboarding

Exercise 5. A lot of fun, not fun at all Everyone has a different idea of fun. For one person, shopping is fun. For another person, shopping is boring, but necessary. Write ten words or phrases from Exercise 4 in one of the columns on page 108. Use your opinion. Add other activities. Then compare your list with a classmate's list.

EXAMPLE:

Not fun	Okay	A lot of fun
stamp collecting	watching TV	making music

In other words, for one of the authors of this book, *stamp collecting is not fun, watching TV is okay,* and *making music is a lot of fun.*

My opinion on leisure activities

Not fun	Okay	A lot of fun

B Structure

Exercise 1. It's good to have friends   Look at the following list of words. Write your opinion **good to have** or **not good to have** after each. Work with a partner and tell each other your opinions.

> **EXAMPLE:**   It's **good to have** a lot of friends. *or*
>
> It's **not good to have** many problems.

Use **a lot of** or **many** with nouns you can count. See Appendix II on page 146 for an explanation of count and noncount nouns.

> **EXAMPLE:**   Some people want **a lot of** friends.
>
> Some people don't think it's good to have **many** friends.

---

1. chances to learn a new sport   _____

2. girlfriends/ boyfriends   _____

3. relatives   _____

4. young brothers and sisters   _____

5. hobbies   _____

6. possessions   _____

Unit 5: Leisure and Recreation

7. televisions in your house   _____

8. experiences in foreign countries   _____

9. difficulties to overcome   _____

10. people who depend on you   _____

Exercise 2. I don't want any problems Everyone wants to avoid problems. We don't want **any** problems in our lives. They make us sad or cause us difficulty. Read the situations that follow. Then write a sentence for each one. Tell what the person didn't want.

> **EXAMPLE:** One boy offered another boy some candy. The boy said, "No, thank you." *He didn't want **any** candy.*

> Use **any** for nouns in the negative when you mean *not one.*
>
> **EXAMPLES:** I have a lot of hobbies. *My brother doesn't have **any** hobbies.*
> I have a lot of free time. *My wife doesn't have **any** free time.*

1. Omar and José were playing soccer. Omar pushed José down. José just walked away.

   José _____

2. Supong tried to tell Kai what card to play. Kai didn't listen to Supong.

   Kai _____

3. Gail gave David a bottle of water while they were running a race. David didn't drink it, and he gave it right back to Gail.

   David _____

4. Maria served her niece, Marta, some cookies and milk. Marta drank the milk, but she didn't eat the cookies.

   Marta _____

5. Thai offered to play piano for Sami when he sang. Sami said he wanted to sing alone.

   Sami _____

6. Jelena offered to teach Stephanie how to ski. Stephanie said she wanted to try by herself.

   Stephanie _____

Write your own situation below. Then tell it to a classmate. Exchange books with your classmate. See if he or she can make a sentence with **any.**

7. _____

_____

_____

Exercise 3. What I have and what I don't have   Think about yourself. Complete the following chart with **much** or **a lot of.**

> Use **a lot of** or **much** for nouns you cannot count. See Appendix II on page 146 for an explanation of count and noncount nouns.
>
> EXAMPLES: Busy people don't have **much** time for having coffee with friends.
>
> People who are not busy may have **a lot of** time for chatting over coffee.

My opinions	
Chance to speak English outside of class	
Ability to play chess	
Time to exercise every day	
Patience with people learning a sport I am good at	

My opinions	
Respect for professional athletes	
Love for music	
Interest in dancing	
Knowledge about opera	
Adventure in my life	
Opportunity to travel to other countries	

 Explain your chart to a classmate.

 Exercise 4. Do they have enough for the party? Abdul and Lars are having a party at their apartment. They have some things they will need for the party, but they don't have other things. You are their party adviser. Look at what they have and tell them if they need more. They are planning a party for twenty people. Complete the chart on page 112 with **enough** whenever possible.

Use **enough** for any noun to show a sufficient amount.

EXAMPLE: That book costs $25.00. I have $30.00 in my wallet. I have **enough** money to buy the book.

What Abdul and Lars have in their apartment	
one table	They don't have enough tables.
six chairs	
a CD player	One CD player is enough.
two dance music CDs and five classical CDs	
two large bottles of soda	
one medium bag of potato chips	
ten glasses	
ten cups	
almost empty carton of milk	
one pound of coffee	
one case of beer	
no pretzels	
two dozen plastic knives and forks	
fifteen paper plates	
three metal spoons	
no deejay	
no sweets	

In your group, look at the preceding chart to see what Abdul and Lars still need. Decide if you want to buy or borrow those items. Fill out the chart that follows and write how much or how many you will buy or borrow.

Party

To buy (how much or how many)	To borrow (how much or how many)

 Exercise 5. Joelle's concert The story of Joelle's concert is missing the words **much, many, any, a lot of,** and **enough.** Read the story on page 114 using one of these words or phrases in the blank spaces to complete the story.

Joelle had played trumpet at ___many___ concerts. However, there is
(1)

one concert she will never forget because she had _____ problems
(2)

on that day. First, she left her house without _____ gas in her car.
(3)

Then she found that there was _____ traffic on the highway.
(4)

What's more, there was so _____ rain that she had trouble seeing
(5)

the road. On the highway, her car stopped because it didn't have

_____ gas in the tank. Joelle got out of her car and walked a mile
(6)

on the highway to get gas, even though there was _____ danger
(7)

because of the traffic and the heavy rain.

When she went to pay for the gas, she found she didn't have

_____ money, only $2.25. She bought one gallon of gas and
(8)

walked back to her car. She drove a few minutes to the place where she

had bought the gas. The few minutes seemed like _____ hours to
(9)

her. The second time she tried to pay with one of her _____
(10)

credit cards, but the gas station didn't take _____ credit cards.
(11)

Joelle had 50¢ left. It was just _____ to call home. When she
(12)

called home, there wasn't _____ body there. She left her wedding
(13)

ring with the gas station owner because she didn't have _____
(14)

money to pay for a full tank of gas. Then she sped off to her concert. She

had to go over the speed limit because she had just _____ time to
(15)

get there. Her dress was soaked with rain, and she didn't have

_____ way to dry herself. She played the concert shivering and
(16)

wet. Before she left the concert hall, she borrowed _____ money
(17)

from her friend, Ellen, a cellist, to pay back the gas station owner. She

drove back to the gas station, paid the gas station owner, took back her

wedding ring, and got home not _____ more than 10 minutes
(18)

late for dinner. The next day she got the flu and was sick in bed for

_____ days after.
(19)

C Writing and Editing

Exercise 1. Inventing the story, part 1 Look at the picture story at the beginning of this chapter. It is about two women and how they have spent time together over many years. Use your imagination to tell their story.

1. What are their names (first and last)?

_____

2. What do they do now?

_____

3. How old were they when they met? How did they meet?

_____

4. What do they enjoy doing together?

_____

Compare your story with your partner's story.

Exercise 2. Inventing the story, part 2 With your partner, use information from Exercise 1 and write a story about the women.

Enjoying Life Together

_____

_____

_____

_____

_____

_____

_____

_____

_____

_____

_____

_____

Exercise 3. Telling your own story Complete the following chart to help you tell the story of how you spend your free time. List at least three different activities.

Activity   What do you do?
Cost   How much does it cost to do?
With whom   Whom do you do it with?
How often   How often do you do it?
Last time   When was the last time you did it?

Activity	Cost	With whom	How often	Last time

 Take turns talking about how you spend your free time.

 Exercise 4. Mapping Choose one of the activities in Exercise 3. Put the name of the activity on the middle line. Put the information about the activity on each radiating line. Talk about your map to your partner.

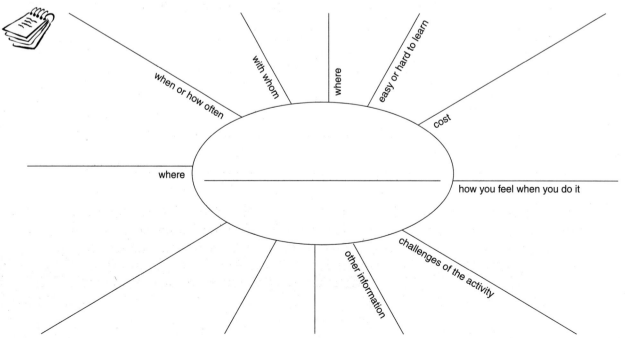

Unit 5: Leisure and Recreation

Exercise 5. Writing about your activity   Use the mind map in Exercise 4 to write a paragraph about your free time activity. The title of your paragraph should use **-ing,** for example, **Skiing, Playing Poker, Shopping.**

Exercise 6. Getting feedback   Exchange books. Read your partner's paragraph and follow the directions below.

1. Is there more information the reader needs to understand the story? If yes, write questions for the writer to answer.

_____

_____

_____

2. Write one comment to the writer about his or her free time activity.

_____

_____

Exercise 7. Writing a second draft Use the feedback from Exercise 6 to help you write a second draft.

D Journal Assignments

Choose one topic each day. Find a place to write outdoors on Monday, Wednesday, and Friday where you can watch people. Find a place to write indoors where there are a lot of people doing things on Tuesday and Thursday.

Monday, Wednesday, Friday

- They're having a good time
- An active person
- An athletic woman
- What to do on a great day

Tuesday, Thursday

- A conversation
- A happy group
- Someone worth watching

UNIT SIX
CHAPTER 11

The Natural World

A Prewriting

Exercise 1. Linking the pictures In each picture below, there are birds. In picture 1, the birds are penguins. In picture 2, the birds are parrots. In picture 3, the birds are pelicans, and in picture 4, the birds are puffins. What is similar about these birds? What is different about them? Where do they live? Make a list of similarities and differences among the birds with your group. Write these similarities and differences on the next page.

Penguin

1.

Parrot

2.

Pelican

3.

Puffin

4.

Similarities among the birds	Differences among the birds

Exercise 2. Creating an alphabet of animals   All of the birds in the pictures begin with the letter **p**: *penguins, parrots, pelicans, puffins.* Below is the English alphabet. See how many animals you know. Work with your partner to think of an animal for each letter of the alphabet.

A	B
C	D
E	F
G	H
I	J
K	L
M	N
O	P
Q	R
S	T
U	V
W	X
Y	Z

Where do these animals live? What is their natural habitat? Tell your partner what you know about each animal.

EXAMPLE: **A** for armadillo. I know that armadillos live in Texas. They live in warm climates. They have a hard shell that covers their bodies.

Exercise 3. Land and sea Draw a line between the animal and its habitat. Use a dictionary if you need help.

EXAMPLE: a. parrots   1. islands
          b. puffins   2. rain forests

Animal	Habitat
a. whale	1. jungle
b. elephant	2. tree
c. frog	3. forest
d. crow	4. bay
e. crocodile	5. stream
f. sheep	6. ocean
g. monkey	7. pond
h. deer	8. field
i. trout	9. meadow
j. scallop	10. river

Add some animals and habitats of your own, from your country or a country that you know.

_____   _____   _____

_____   _____   _____

  Now tell your partner about the animals and their habitats.

EXAMPLE: Penguins live in Antarctica.
          Parrots live in the rain forest that borders the Amazon River.
          Pelicans live near the seashore, where the land meets the water.
          Puffins live on isolated islands in the North Sea.

Exercise 4. A day in the life Choose one of the birds in the pictures. Think about its daily activities. What does it do? What does it eat? Where does it get food? Does it live alone? Where does it live? If you are having difficulty answering these questions, use an encyclopedia or go online to search the Internet.

Notes	
bird	
habitat	
food	
activities	

Each person in your group should have a different bird to talk about. Take turns telling the story of each bird. Make notes on the ones your classmates talk about.

Notes

Exercise 5. Pets, cows, and wild creatures The birds in the pictures all live freely in nature. They are *wild animals.* Animals that we bring into our homes and train to live near us or with us are *tame animals.* These animals are our *pets.* They usually don't work. We keep them for company. Other animals, like *horses* and *burros,* work for us. And some animals, like *cows* and *pigs,* we raise for food.

Put the animals below into one of the categories in the chart: *wild, pet, work,* or *food.* Some animals can be in more than one category. For example, a dog can both be a pet and work animal. Then add other animals to each category.

pig   canary   cat   rattlesnake   gorilla

chicken   monkey   plow horse

fox

guide dog   turkey   deer   eagle

sheep   goldfish

Wild animals	Pets	Work animals	Food animals

B Structure

Exercise 1. Describing animals—definitions   Here are definitions for the birds in the pictures.

1. A penguin is a large black and white sea bird **that** cannot fly.

2. A parrot is a colorful bird with a large beak **that** lives in the tropics.

3. A pelican is a water bird **that** catches fish in its large beak.

4. A puffin is a black and white bird **that** breeds on isolated rock formations in the sea.

> These sentences are definitions. Notice how they use the word **that.** To combine two sentences with **that,** replace the subject of the second sentence with **that.**
>
> **EXAMPLE:**   A penguin is a large black and white sea bird.
>
> A penguin cannot fly.
>
> *A penguin is a large black and white sea bird **that** cannot fly.*

Now go back to Prewriting Exercises 2, 3, and 5 to reread the names of the animals in those exercises. Choose four animals and write a definition for each one.

1. _____

2. _____

3. _____

4. _____

Read your definitions to your partner. Help each other correct any mistakes in your definitions.

Exercise 2. Which would you choose? Imagine that you have a choice of things. Ask your partner to make a choice. Write his or her answer and your own answer. Answer without using **that**.

EXAMPLE: You can live on an island **that is** near Antarctica or on an island **(that is)** in the South Pacific Ocean. Which would you like?

I would like to live on an island near Antarctica.

That is optional in sentences with the verb **be.** The verb must also be removed if **that** is removed.

EXAMPLE: an island that is near Antarctica

an island near Antarctica

---

1. You can have a dog trained to hunt or one trained to do tricks. Which would you choose?

    Partner _____   Self _____

2. You can study sea birds near the coast of Africa or near the coast of South America. Which would you choose?

    Partner _____   Self _____

3. You can live for a month on a ranch in Alaska or in New Zealand. Which would you choose?

    Partner _____   Self _____

4. You can travel to Australia or a country in Europe. Which would you choose?

    Partner _____   Self _____

5. You can work for an organization concerned with human rights or the environment. Which would you choose?

    Partner _____   Self _____

6. You can stay at a camp near the seashore or in the mountains. Which would you choose?

    Partner _____   Self _____

Exercise 3. I would like to Each of the answers in Exercise 2 can be rewritten as a sentence with **I would like to.**

> EXAMPLE: an island near Antarctica
>
> I would like to visit an island near Antarctica.

Rewrite each of your personal choices in Exercise 2 with **I would like to.**

> EXAMPLES: I would like to visit an island near Antarctica. *or*
>
> I would like to visit an island **that is** near Antarctica.

1. _____
2. _____
3. _____
4. _____
5. _____
6. _____

C Writing and Editing

Exercise 1. Categorizing birds Look at the following list of birds. You should use a dictionary to help you put them into categories according to your thinking. You may have fewer than four groups. You may have more than four groups. The important thing is to have a reason to put the birds into groups.

albatross	penguin	turkey	duck	chicken
sparrow	robin	quail	woodpecker	seagull
eagle	hawk	hummingbird	parrot	pelican
pigeon	crow	falcon	goose	flamingo
pheasant	vulture	parakeet	toucan	

Group 1	Group 2	Group 3	Group 4

Exercise 2. Describing why things go together For each group of birds in Exercise 1, write a sentence that describes what all the birds in the group have in common, why they go together.

EXAMPLES: All of the birds live near the water.

All of the birds in this group have beautiful colors.

Group 1 _____

_____

Group 2 _____

_____

Group 3 _____

_____

Group 4 _____

_____

Read the list of birds to the people in your group. After you read the list, ask the other students to guess what your sentence will say. Then read your sentence to the group.

Exercise 3. Writing a paragraph of classification   Now you are ready to write the first draft of a paragraph that divides birds into different groups. Include examples of each group of birds.

_____

Exercise 4. Writing beginnings—topic sentences   Look at the paragraph that you wrote in Exercise 3. Is there a good beginning? Did you write something at the beginning to get your reader interested and to give the main idea of your paragraph? A sentence that interests the reader and gives the main or controlling idea of the paragraph is called a **topic sentence.** A topic sentence is often at the beginning of a single paragraph.

EXAMPLES: Birds are in the air, on the land, and under the sea.

How are birds different from each other?*

Birds can be divided into groups according to how people understand them.

What do a sparrow, a puffin, a vulture, and a duck have in common?*

People think of birds as small flying creatures, but that is only partly true.

"Free as a bird" is an expression that is not completely true.

* Notice that these questions do not give us the main ideas. Instead, they give us something to think about. We need to read more to see how the questions will be answered.

Unit 6: The Natural World

Which sentences do you like? Why? Does your paragraph have a good beginning? If it does not, or if you want to change your beginning sentence, write a sentence for your paragraph below.

_____

_____

Exercise 5. Endings—concluding sentences   Readers are attracted to interesting beginnings, and they are pleased by thoughtful endings. Sometimes beginnings are good places to start with questions, but questions can also be good endings, good **conclusions.**

>   **EXAMPLES:**   Do you notice the birds all around you every day?
>
>   Have you ever wanted to be a bird?
>
>   What other animal has so captured our imaginations?

Write a question ending for your paragraph.

_____

_____

General statements also make good **conclusions.**

>   **EXAMPLES:**   The many different kinds of birds make the lives of human beings richer.
>
>   Birds are as different as people are.
>
>   Everywhere you go, you will find birds.

Now write a general statement about birds.

_____

_____

Exercise 6. Rewriting your paragraph   Rewrite your paragraph about birds on a sheet of paper. Make sure that you have a strong beginning and a strong ending.

D Journal Assignment

Choose one of the following topics to write about.

- Become a bird watcher. Look out your window. What birds do you see? Write down their names and what they do. Look out your window in the morning, in the afternoon, at night. Are the same birds there? Write about them.

- Think of the last time you ate a bird. What was it? A chicken? A duck? A goose? A pheasant? Write about that time. How was the bird prepared? Who bought it? Who killed it? How did it taste?

- Think of animals that eat birds. Think of animals that birds eat. Write about them.

- If you were a bird, which bird would you be? Write about it.

- Have you ever had a bird as a pet? Do you know of someone who has a bird as a pet now? What is it like to take care of a bird? Write about it.

The Natural World

A Prewriting

Exercise 1. Here or there?   Look at the following words and pictures. Write the number of the picture that contains the word's meaning next to the word.

_____ apartment building		_____ traffic	
_____ wild animals		_____ running stream	
_____ farm animals		_____ meadow	
_____ cows		_____ sidewalk	
_____ horses		_____ dirty streets	
_____ farmhouse		_____ polluted air	
_____ store		_____ noisy	
_____ telephone lines		_____ suburban	
_____ power lines		_____ country	
_____ house		_____ urban	
_____ barn		_____ dirt road	

1.

2.

3.

4.

Exercise 2. Where you live   Think about the place where you were born. Which picture is most like that place? Why?

Did you live in . . .   the country or the city?

a dirty area or a clean area?

a crowded, noisy area or an empty, quiet area?

an apartment or a house?

How else can you describe where you live? Make notes below.

_____

_____

_____

_____

_____

 Now each person takes a turn telling about where he or she comes from.

Exercise 3. Where would you like to live?   Draw a picture below of the place you would like to live.

Exchange pictures. Try to guess what kind of place your partner wants to live in. Is it a place you know? Ask your partner about it.

Exercise 4. What happened?   The picture story is about one place. It shows what happened over time. Look at the pictures. Write down below what you see in the first picture. Then write how it changed in the next picture. Continue with each picture in this way.

PICTURE ONE _____

_____

PICTURE TWO _____

_____

PICTURE THREE _____

_____

PICTURE FOUR _____

_____

Exercise 5. Looking out the window, walking out the door— a quick write   Think about the place where you are now. Then look out the window or walk out the door and sit somewhere outside. Imagine this place 100 years ago, 1,000 years ago, 100,000 years ago.

- What did it look like?

- What kinds of plants and trees were there?

- What kinds of animals were there?

- Was there water or was it dry?

- Was it hot or was it cold?

- Were human beings present? If they were, what did they look like?

Write what you see here.

_____

_____

_____

_____

_____

_____

_____

_____

_____

_____

B Structure

Exercise 1. Describing in detail   Look at the sentences below. Each sentence has the same subject. All four sentences can be made into one by adding only the different words from sentences 2, 3, and 4 to the first sentence. Combine the following groups of sentences. Follow the example.

EXAMPLE: 1. The road was *long*.

2. The road was *dark*.

3. The road was *bumpy*.

4. The road was *difficult to drive on*.

The long, dark, bumpy road was difficult to drive on.

1. The stream was pretty.

The stream was little.

The stream was fast-moving.

The stream was safe to drink from.

_____

2. The bear was huge.

The bear was brown.

The bear was female.

The bear was feeding her cub.

_____

3. The farmhouse was old.

The farmhouse was red.

The farmhouse was broken-down.

The farmhouse was the home to a family of field mice.

_____

4. The pig was fat.

   The pig was pink.

   The pig was oinking.

   The pig was rolling around in the mud.

   _____

5. The meadow was beautiful.

   The meadow was quiet.

   The meadow was green.

   The meadow was replaced by houses.

   _____

6. The power lines are long.

   The power lines are ugly.

   The power lines are black.

   The power lines made the place depressing.

   _____

7. The sidewalks are busy.

   The sidewalks are dirty.

   The sidewalks are cracked.

   The sidewalks show the change from country to town.

   _____

8. The city is dirty.

   The city is noisy.

   The city is polluted.

   The city is a difficult place to live.

   _____

Exercise 2. Mixing and matching words to form descriptive phrases Choose a word from the rows and make a phrase. Use at least four rows. Write five phrases. Do not use a comma after the last adjective.

EXAMPLE: an ugly, big, heavy, sleepy, old, green frog

beautiful	small	round	tired	old	red	sea
ugly	big	square	sleepy	young	white	frog
useless	tiny	thin	energetic	ancient	black	forest
deadly	huge	heavy	sick	newborn	yellow	animal
common	tall		healthy	adult	brown	mountain
rare	short			baby	green	desert

1. _____

2. _____

3. _____

4. _____

5. _____

Exercise 3. One day I went out walking Practice the phrases in Exercise 2 with these words: *One day I went out walking, and I saw . . .*

EXAMPLE: One day I went out walking, and I saw a small, healthy, green frog.

Take turns dictating two sentences to each other in your group. Write the sentences your group dictates below. Then practice saying them three times each at normal speed.

1. _____

2. _____

3. _____

4. _____

5. _____

6. _____

Exercise 4. Counting nature Look at these words from nature. Imagine that you are outdoors. You are looking around you. What do you see?

EXAMPLE: I see dark clouds. I smell fresh air.

clouds	*a meadow*	*air*	*sunshine*
stars	*waves*	*grass*	*a stream*
water	*lightning*	*thunder*	*rain*
snow	*wind*	*leaves*	*dirt*

1. I see _____.

2. I hear _____.

3. I smell _____.

4. I see _____.

5. I see _____.

6. I hear _____.

Now go to one of your favorite local places where you are surrounded by nature. Write what you see.

_____

_____

_____

_____

_____

_____

_____

_____

_____

_____

_____

C Writing and Editing

Exercise 1. Writing to remember   Write down as many things as you can remember about the picture story at the beginning of this unit. Try not to look back at the picture story.

_____

_____

_____

_____

_____

_____

_____

_____

Exercise 2. Using past work to write a new paragraph   Look back at Part A, Exercise 4 in which you listed the changes from one picture to the next. Use that information and the ideas you just wrote down in Exercise 1. Write a paragraph about how the area in the pictures has changed.

_____

_____

_____

_____

_____

_____

_____

_____

_____

_____

_____

_____

_____

Unit 6: The Natural World

Give your paragraph to a partner to read. Ask your partner to write a title for your paragraph. Write the title below.

_____

Exercise 3. Swapping sentences   Work with the same partner as in Exercise 2. First, find a sentence in your partner's paragraph that you like. Second, put it into your own paragraph. Then, your partner will pick a sentence from your paragraph and put it into his or her story. Finally, reread your paragraph. Does it sound good to you? If not, find another partner. Follow the steps in the sentence swap. Continue swapping sentences until you have the story you want.

Exercise 4. Redrafting your paragraph   Read your paragraph to the group without interruption. Read slowly. Read clearly. Read with expression. Try to get your listeners interested in your story.

Ask for feedback. *Feedback* is the reaction other students give to you about your story. Here are some questions to help with feedback.

- What did you like in the story?

- What sounded good?

- What was not clear?

- Did you feel that the paragraph had an ending?

- Did the paragraph interest you?

- Did it make you think?

Use your group's feedback to write a second draft of your paragraph on the next page.

_____

_____

_____

_____

_____

_____

_____

_____

_____

_____

_____

_____

D Journal Assignment

Think about the times in your life when you were impressed by the power or the beauty of nature. Have you ever experienced . . .?

- a heavy snowstorm
- a monsoon
- a drought
- a flood
- a wild fire
- an earthquake

- a tidal wave
- a landslide
- an avalanche
- a heat wave
- a cold spell

Write in your journal about your experiences with nature.

Appendix I

Nouns, Verbs, and Pronouns

- A **noun** is a person, place or thing. Things can be abstract, nonmaterial. For example, *truth* and *beauty* are nouns.

    EX.   that **student, Mr. Smith, you** (*person*)

    New York City, my **room,** the **gym** (*place*)

    a good **book,** our **dog,** his final exam **grade** (*thing*)

- A **verb** is an action or a state of being.

    EX.   eat, sleep, think (*action*)

    seem, feel, be (*state of being*)

- Some verbs combine with other verbs to create meaning with verb tense. They are **auxiliary verbs.**

    EX.   He **is** going to the concert.

    Moira **has** seen that movie.

- A **pronoun** takes the place of a noun.

    noun   pronoun
    EX.   My **teacher** is a nice person. **She** is a nice person.

Appendix II

Types of Nouns

- Nouns are first divided into common nouns and proper nouns.

    EX.   common nouns: water, school, baby, toy

    proper nouns: Dave, Mrs. Milton, Illinois, Mexico

- Some common nouns are countable.

    EX.   a glass, a classroom, a baby

- Some common nouns are not countable.

    EX.   milk, water, homework, chocolate

- You can count noncount nouns by using a containing word or a counting word before them.

    EX.   glass of milk, a gallon of water, a lot of homework, a piece of chocolate.

- Some common nouns represent more than one thing or more than one person.

    EX.   class, team, crew, family

- Collective nouns can take either plural or singular forms of the verb to reflect how the writer thinks about the noun.

    EX.   The family is gone. *(the whole family)*

    The family are busy with holiday preparations. *(each one in the family)*

Appendix III

The Traditional Twelve Verb Tenses

English has twelve tenses according to many traditional grammar books. They are in chart form below.

Aspect → Time ↓	Simple	Perfect	Progressive (or continuous)	Perfect Progressive
past	John **saw** a good movie.	John **had seen** the movie (before he read the book).	John **was watching** TV (when the doorbell rang).	John **had been watching** TV (when the fire started).
present	John **reads** poetry.	John **has seen** that movie.	John **is watching** TV.	John **has been watching** TV all day long.
future	John **will read** the report tomorrow.	John **will have seen** that movie (before it leaves town).	John **will be watching** TV (when I get home).	John **will have been watching** TV for ten hours by midnight.

Common Verb Spelling Rules and Irregular Verbs

Spelling Rules for Simple Present Tense—Third Person

- For most verbs, add **-s**

  EX. He work**s**.

- Verbs that end in **-y** change to **-ies**.

  EX. She stud**ies**.

  He tr**ies**.

- Verbs that end in a vowel followed by **-y** do not change to **-ies**.

  EX. He pla**ys**.

  She sa**ys**.

Spelling Rules for Present Continuous Tense

- One-syllable verbs that are *consonant + vowel + consonant* double the final consonant.

get	getting
run	running

- Verbs that end in a consonant and **-e,** drop the **-e.**

drive	driving
make	making

Spelling Rules for Simple Past Tense

- For most regular verbs, add **-ed.**

work	worked
talk	talked

- For words ending in *consonant +* **y,** change the **y** to **i** and add **-ed.**

study	studied
try	tried

- Words ending in *vowel +* **y** follow the rule of regular verbs.

play	played
enjoy	enjoyed

- Words ending with *consonant(s) + vowel + consonant* double the last consonant and add **-ed.**

plan	planned
shop	shopped

Common Irregular Verb Forms

Base Form	Irregular Past Form	Irregular Past Participles
be	was, were	been
become	became	become
begin	began	begun
break	broke	broken
bring	brought	brought
buy	bought	bought
come	came	come
do	did	done
eat	ate	eaten
get	got	gotten
give	gave	given
go	went	gone
grow	grew	grown
find	found	found
forget	forgot	forgotten
know	knew	known
have	had	had
hear	heard	heard
hurt	hurt	hurt
keep	kept	kept
leave	left	left
make	made	made
put	put	put

(Continued)

Base Form	Irregular Past Form	Irregular Past Participles
read	read	read
ride	rode	ridden
run	ran	run
say	said	said
see	saw	seen
sell	sold	sold
send	sent	sent
sit	sat	sat
speak	spoke	spoken
stand	stood	stood
take	took	taken
teach	taught	taught
tell	told	told
think	thought	thought
understand	understood	understood
wear	wore	worn
write	wrote	written

Writing to Learn: *The Paragraph*

Appendix IV

Adjectives

An **adjective** is a word that describes a noun or pronoun. Most adjectives come before the noun or pronoun that they describe. However, adjectives may also come after the noun or pronoun they describe, particularly with a form of the verb *be.*

EX. 1. What color car do you drive?

adjective
I drive a **red** car.

2. How many students are in the class?

adjective
Sixteen students.

3. Which of these do you want?

adjective*
I want **that** one.

* This, that, these, and those are often called demonstrative adjectives because they demonstrate or indicate which item you are talking about.

4. How is that teacher?

form of *be* adjective**
That teacher *is* pretty **good.**

** This is a post-nominal adjective. It comes after the noun it describes.

Appendix V

Sentence Order: Subject, Verb, Object

- Every sentence in English has a subject and a verb. Subjects are often the first noun in a sentence. Verbs often follow the subject.

        subject   verb
    EX.   Alison cooks.

- Many sentences have objects. Objects are usually nouns or noun phrases that follow the verb.

        subject   verb   object (noun phrase)
    EX.   Alison cooks Italian food.

- The most common word order in simple English sentences is **subject, verb, object.**

Appendix VI

Basic Capitalization

- Every sentence begins with a capital letter.

    EX.   **T**his is an important rule.

- The pronoun **I** is always capitalized.
    EX.   She said that **I** did it.

- Days of the week and months begin with a capital letter.
    EX.   **M**onday, **T**uesday, **M**arch, **A**pril

- People's titles begin with a capital letter.
    EX.   Let me introduce you to **D**r. Jones and **P**rofessor McDoodle.

- Towns, cities, countries, nationalities, and languages begin with capital letters.
    EX.   **C**anterbury, **R**ussia, **M**exican, **I**talian

Appendix VII

Basic Form of a Paragraph

The basic form of a paragraph follows these rules:

- Indent at the beginning of a paragraph.

- Leave a margin on the left and on the right.

- Use 1.5 or 2 for line spacing when word processing, or skip a line when writing longhand.

- Use one space after a comma and two spaces after a period when word processing. When writing longhand, be sure to leave space after a period to separate sentences.

- One sentence follows another with no space in between.

EX.

When I was a little boy, my mother used to walk me to school. She told me never to cross the busy city streets by myself. My school was only two blocks away from my home, but my mother used to say, "Don't cross those streets by yourself. It's too dangerous." So, I listened to her.

One day my mother was sick. She asked a friend's mother to stop by our house and take me to school. The woman forgot about me. My mother was sick in bed, but she started to dress. I said, "Mom, you're too sick to take me. I'm big enough to cross by myself." That was the first time I crossed a city street by myself. I was 5 years old.

Appendix VIII

Journal Writing

Journals are notebooks in which writers keep a record of ideas, opinions, and descriptions of daily life. Journals help writers develop their creativity. In writing classes, instructors often ask students to write in journals.

Each writing instructor has different ideas about journal writing. Your instructor will tell you how to keep your journal and will probably collect it at certain times during the semester. Your instructor may write reactions to what you write and offer suggestions for vocabulary or improving your grammar. The main point of keeping a journal as a language student is to give you a chance to write about your ideas without worrying about a grade or correct grammar and usage. Journal writing is practice in writing and thinking.

Buy a standard size notebook with lined paper. Make this notebook your journal for this writing class only. Write nothing else in it. Do not write other class assignments in your journal. There are many rewards from keeping a journal, in addition to the informal conversation that takes place in it between you and yourself, and you and your instructor: when you have finished the course, you will have a record of what you read, what you experienced, and what you thought about during that time.

At the end of each chapter in this book, you will find some topics related to the theme of the unit. Write about them in your journal.

Glossary of Grammatical Terms

base form The base form is also called the simple form. It is the infinitive without *to*. Example: *go*

consonant In writing, a consonant is any letter of the English alphabet except *a, e, i, o,* and *u*. In speech, a consonant sound is one in which the air from the lungs is blocked slightly to greatly by the tongue, teeth, lips, and shape of the inside of the mouth. (The inside of the mouth is called the *oral cavity* in speech science. Nasal consonant sounds are made by blocking the air stream from coming out of the oral cavity. It is redirected through the *nasal cavity*.)

English consonants *b, c, d, f, g, h, j, k, l, m, n, p, q, r, s, t, v, w, x, y*, z*

demonstrative adjectives *this, that, these, those*

negation Changing affirmative to negative. Examples: *She **isn't** here. I **don't** work. They**'re not** going. They have**n't** been.*

object The receiver of an action. It is a noun. Example: *He gave the book to his **sister**.*

object pronouns *me, you, him, her, it, us, them*

past participle The verb form used in perfect tenses. Regular past participles end in **ed.** There are many irregular past participles.

plural Plural indicates more than one. Examples: *books, children, women*

possessive adjectives *my, your, his, her, its, our, their*

preposition These are words that show location, direction, and time. Examples: *to, in, at, on, from, over*

prepositional phrase A prepositional phrase is a group of words beginning with a preposition. Examples: ***in** high school, **to** the store*

pronouns Pronouns take the place of nouns. Example: ***My sister** (noun) is a singer. **She** (pronoun) is a singer.*

question word order The normal word order for questions is (Question word) verb + subject or (Question word) auxiliary verb + subject + verb. Examples: *Where was he? Where did he go? Did he go?*

question words *who(m), what, when, where, which, why, how, how long*

singular Singular means only one. Examples: *book, child, woman*

statement word order Normal word order for statements is subject + verb (+ object). Example: *I love English.*

subject Every sentence has a subject and verb. The subject tells who or what is doing or experiencing something. Example: ***I** come from China.*

subject pronouns *I, you, he, she, it, we, they*

verb Every sentence has a subject and verb. The verb tells what the subject is doing or experiencing. Example: *He **comes** from China.*

vowel In writing, the vowel letters are *a, e, i, o, u* and sometimes the letter *y.** In speech, a vowel sound is one in which the air from the lungs flows freely through the oral cavity or nasal cavity.

* The letter *y* sometimes acts as a vowel in writing and in speech. For example: *Egypt, rhythm, any.*